ATONEMENT
AND THE
LIFE OF FAITH

Adam J. Johnson

Baker Academic
a division of Baker Publishing Group
Grand Rapids, Michigan

Published by Baker Academic
a division of Baker Publishing Group
Grand Rapids, Michigan
BakerAcademic.com

Printed in the United States of America

Library of Congress Cataloging-in-Publication Data
Names: Johnson, Adam J., author.
Title: Atonement and the life of faith / Adam J. Johnson.
Description: Grand Rapids, Michigan : Baker Academic, a division of Baker Publishing Group,
    [2024] | Series: Soteriology and doxology | Includes bibliographical references and index.
Identifiers: LCCN 2024011523 | ISBN 9781540961709 (paperback) | ISBN 9781540968326
    (casebound) | ISBN 9781493421985 (pdf) | ISBN 9781493421992 (ebook)
Subjects: LCSH: Atonement. | Christian life. | Public worship. | Theology, Doctrinal.
Classification: LCC BT265.3 .J635 2024 | DDC 234/.5—dc23/eng/20240412
LC record available at https://lccn.loc.gov/2024011523

24   25   26   27   28   29   30   7   6   5   4   3   2   1

I dedicate this book
to the faculty, staff, and students
of the Torrey Honors College
at Biola University.

When asked about what I do for work, I often say,
"I am retired and just doing what I love."

Contents

Series Preface

And Moses said, "Here I am."

Exodus 3:4

IN THE WILDERNESS, Moses stumbles upon a burning bush that somehow goes unconsumed. As if the scene is not arresting enough, the God of his forefathers bellows forth from that crackling, glowing bush: "Moses, Moses!" The response of Moses is simple and yet so evocative of a faithful response to God's call: "Here I am." Holy Scripture pictures that response time and again. So many other encounters with God are unmistakably echoed and foreshadowed here: Samuel, Mary, Jesus, and of course Adam. To Adam, God calls, "Where are you?" and he hides, and his hiding is paradigmatic of us all, sadly (Gen. 3:8–10); *but* Moses, Samuel, Mary, and Jesus *offer themselves* in response to the gracious calling of God: "Here I am, Lord." Their proclamation inspires what this series humbly attempts to accomplish: theological activity that bears witness to God's work in time and space to redeem and restore by following the doxological pattern of Moses. Addressed by God and fearful to look upon God's face, Moses finds himself suddenly shoeless in God's holy presence.

Said more formally, the volumes in the Soteriology and Doxology series offer specifically theological interpretations of the Christian life through the lens of various features of God's gracious activity to save, in which doctrinal activity is suffused with and held together by praise. The *gracious acts of God* are the contemplative aim of the series, advancing Christian rationality in grateful response to the redemptive, restorative, and transformative work of the Father by the Son and the Spirit. Focusing on soteriological loci, the topics addressed follow a twofold inclination: that God is the ever-present, captivating reality of all theological work, and that this focus awakens a doxological response that is intrinsic to the proper mode of theological reflection. As such, the orientation of each volume is both dogmatic *and* doxological: each particular doctrine is located within an attentive retrieval of the Christian confession, all while demonstrating how theological reflection springs from worship and spills over into prayer and praise. Seeking to be catholic and evangelical, this series draws upon the richness of the whole church while keeping the sufficiency and singularity of the gospel at center.

The books in the series are designed for theologians-in-formation, meaning that the pedagogical aim of each volume is to train student-readers in a form of theological reasoning that unites what often remains painfully separate in Christian theology: doctrine and spirituality, theology and prayer, the church and the academy, the body of Christ and the individual theologian. This series' approach to theology is exemplified by men and women across the Christian tradition, from Athanasius to Benedict, Ephrem the Syrian to Anselm, Bonaventure to Catherine of Siena, and Aquinas to Calvin. However, with the inclusion of theology in the academic disciplines of the modern university, the expectations and norms of theological reasoning have been altered in many quarters: exegesis is sequestered from theology, and dogmatics from doxology. This series offers something different. It seeks to retrieve forms of theological reflection unapologetic about their home within Christian worship and celebratory of their place within the entire Christian tradition.

With the sight of God as the proper aim of theological contemplation—trembling before the descending fire that calls us to bear witness to his presence—each volume seeks to constructively articulate soteriological loci through the broad range of biblical, historical, and contemporary issues with an eye to expositing the Christian life. While the different authors will vary in how they approach these tasks, the overall flow of each volume will follow a broad fivefold movement: (1) creed, (2) scriptural range, (3) comparative soteriology, (4) constructive theology, and (5) the Christian life, along with a doxological prelude and doxological interludes throughout. Having approached the doctrine from the standpoint of the *regula fidei* through creedal reflection; looked to Holy Scripture for the doctrine's content, scope, and form; and measured diverse traditions of biblical interpretation and theological reasoning, each volume offers a contemporary restatement of Christian teaching that shows how this theological locus directs doxology and Christian living. The *lived* reality of Christian existence, often far from the purview of theological reflection, remains the focused end of articulating the saving acts of God.

O the depth of the riches and wisdom and knowledge of God! . . .
For from him and through him and to him are all things. To him be
the glory forever. Amen. (Rom. 11:33, 36)

Kent Eilers
Kyle C. Strobel
Series Editors

Preface

Can you be Holy without accomplishing the end for which you are created? Can you be Divine unless you be Holy? Can you accomplish the end for which you were created, unless you be Righteous? Can you then be Righteous, unless you be just in rendering to Things their due esteem? All things were made to be yours; and you were made to prize them according to their value: which is your office and duty, the end for which you were created, and the means whereby you enjoy. The end for which you were created, is that by prizing all that God hath done, you may enjoy yourself and Him in Blessedness.

Thomas Traherne, *Centuries of Meditations* 1.12

THIS IS A BOOK ABOUT THE ATONEMENT—about the meaning and significance of the death and resurrection of Jesus. But it is, at the same time, about two other things. First and foremost, it is a book about worship; second, it is a book about the "third article." Paul tells us:

I appeal to you therefore, brothers and sisters, by the mercies of God, to present your bodies as a living sacrifice, holy and acceptable to God, which is your spiritual worship. Do not be conformed to this world, but be transformed by the renewal of your mind, that by testing you

may discern what is the will of God, what is good and acceptable and
perfect. (Rom. 12:1–2)

There are several remarkable features about this passage. First, Paul
integrates the atonement via the notion of sacrifice and worship. Second, Paul integrates the physical and the spiritual; presenting our
bodies properly just is our "spiritual" or "reasonable" worship (τὴν
λογικὴν λατρείαν ὑμῶν). And third, the transformation in question,
the shift from being conformed to the world to being holy and acceptable to God, occurs by means of the renewal of our minds. To weave
these points together, it is precisely by a proper kind of knowing, of
a renewal of our minds, that we become the kinds of creatures who
worship God properly—a worship that entails lives of living sacrifice.
The mind and proper worship are utterly and completely interwoven.

And while we have already seen that this proper kind of knowing
connects to the doctrine of the atonement in Paul's mind (through
the notion of living sacrifice), the connection is yet stronger. For how
exactly do we renew our minds? To jump to another passage in Paul:
"And I, when I came to you, brothers and sisters, did not come proclaiming to you the testimony of God with lofty speech or wisdom.
For I decided to know nothing among you except Jesus Christ and
him crucified" (1 Cor. 2:1–2). Paul is able to distill his ministry, his
posture toward the Corinthian church, to one thing: knowing Christ
and him crucified. Now, of course, given Paul's pattern of thought,
this likewise entails the resurrection and the way that this shapes
the whole history of God's covenantal relationship with Israel—and
through them, creation as a whole. But Paul can nevertheless say that
he knows just one thing.

The doctrine of the atonement, in other words, is the hinge upon
which we are to become different kinds of creatures—creatures able
to properly worship the maker of heaven and earth. The doctrine
of the atonement, and therefore this book, is fundamentally about
worship, as we seek to conform our minds and thus our whole selves
to the reality of Christ's death and resurrection.

Does the goal of worship change in any way how we go about the theological task, how I write this book? I believe it does. First, it means that this book should be about God—not about me or culture or perceived problems or polemics or anything of the sort. Of course, these may have their proper place. But order and priority are vital to keeping all things, books included, healthy. So this book should be first and foremost about God. And for this reason, it should be joyful. God's work, as revealed in Holy Scripture, is not entirely positive. God destroys. God kills. God judges. But fundamentally, God's work in, through, and for Jesus Christ—and in Jesus Christ for us—is good news. So this book is (or should be) fundamentally joyful. For that reason, I spend far more time saying what I believe to be true rather than critiquing false views. I choose proclamation over polemic. The fear is more that I sin by omission, leaving out or precluding some aspect of the work of Christ, than that I make a misstep and say something false. The posture is more joyful than defensive in this way. And because it is joyful, it finds room or freedom to be playful and creative. There are places or chapters in the book where I venture into areas of the doctrine that have been relatively undeveloped in its history—not to be sensational but because when we work or act out of joy, more of our faculties, more of our creativity, enters into the service of our work. Theology that worships tends to be free and creative theology—but no less orthodox for all that.

Second, this is a book about the "third article." The Apostles' Creed is often referred to in terms of three articles; the first is about the Father, the second about the incarnate Son, and the third about the Holy Spirit and things particularly related to the Spirit: church, eschatology, and so forth. In my previous books on the doctrine of the atonement, I focus on the first two articles: some of the ways in which the doctrines of the Trinity, of the divine attributes, of election, of Christology, and so on shape our thinking about the doctrine of the atonement. The emphasis in this book is on the last part of the Apostles' Creed, on the church and its history, the Holy Spirit, forgiveness, and healing. The possible exception to this is the chapter on Scripture, but there, too, I am thinking about how to be guided in reading Scripture well by the teaching and pattern of the church. This is not to say that the atonement can and should be understood exclusively from the standpoint of the third article—far from it! But the standpoint is a good and proper one that has opened up new and beautiful ways in my own life for understanding the saving work of Jesus Christ, and I hope you will likewise benefit.

This is, then, a book about worship and about the Holy Spirit and the church, or to put it more poetically, it is about the Holy Spirit in the church, guiding and shaping its participation in the worship proper to the eternal life of God.

Acknowledgments

IN THINKING THROUGH THE FOLKS I would like to acknowledge for their part in the writing of this book, I am mostly struck by the role of friendship in my life and how naturally interwoven it is into my scholarship. Dave Nelson was first a friend and then the editor supervising this series—but our conversations about family and theology (usually in that order) came first. And when Bob Hosack took over the series, that too was first a friendship. Matt Jenson, at a conference, told me, "That guy is really cool." I walked over to the man who turned out to be Bob, told him a friend said he was cool, and only later, over coffee, found out he was a publisher. Thanks to both Dave and Bob for their work on this book and the series as a whole.

I dedicate the book to the faculty, staff, and students of the Torrey Honors College, where I teach, and it is those friendships that shape so much of what and how I write. The conversations among the faculty theologians (Matt Jenson, Greg Peters, Ryan Peterson, and Fred Sanders), sometimes in my office and sometimes in my backyard, bear consistent fruit in so many different ways. The friendships across the faculty as a whole create an environment in which the life of the mind is in service of the triune God and a matter of joy, creativity, and freedom rather than one of pressure or competition. When your boss (Paul Spears) and your dean (Melissa Johnson) happen to be your friends, and when scholars in other disciplines are first and foremost friends with intellectual and disciplinary tools that only make your own work better and richer (everyone should have at least one historian like Todd Thompson in their life), then work, research, and play easily blend together, to the benefit of all.

The same holds true of my students (and alumni) in the Torrey Honors College at Biola University and the Masters in Classical Theology at Talbot Theological Seminary. The blending of teaching, mentoring, and friendship we get to have with our students in class, office hours, or in the summer national parks trip/class my wife and I teach creates a rich network of relationships that is so nourishing to the theological work I do. The chapter in this book that I cowrote with one of my former students, Tessa Hayashida, bears witness to that.

And of course there is the wider network of friendships, nourished by theological conferences, that I find so helpful. Time with Mike Allen, Matt Anderson, Marc Cortez, Steve Duby, Matthias Grebe, Scott Harrower, Han-luen Kantzer Komline, Matthew Levering, David Luy, David Moffitt, Paul Nimmo, Scott and Laura Rosenkranz, Kate Sonderegger, Adonis Vidu, Tom Ward, and too many others to count is at the heart of my research and writing.

In addition, I am grateful for a sabbatical and a couple of research and development grants from Biola University, for the opportunity from Kent Eilers and Kyle Strobel to write this book, for the incredible editorial work by the team at Baker (Brandon Benziger and Tim West), and for my research assistant, Sierra Christensen. Thanks to Daniel Joseph and Sierra Volmar for compiling the indexes.

Writing theology is something I do as matter of joy and worship of the risen Lord Jesus Christ, in service of the church, and as part of the broader Christian life. Permeating that life is the life of my family. I am so grateful that my work as a theologian is part and parcel of my marriage to Katrina and the way we raise our boys, Reuben, Nathan, and Simeon. And that life, of course, is so greatly shaped by the larger membership of which we are a part and for which we are so grateful.

Abbreviations

ANF	*Ante-Nicene Fathers*
CCSG	Corpus Christianorum: Series Graeca
CD	Karl Barth, *Church Dogmatics*
CWS	Classics of Western Spirituality
FC	Fathers of the Church
Institutes	John Calvin, *Institutes of the Christian Religion*
NICOT	New International Commentary on the Old Testament
NPNF[2]	*Nicene and Post-Nicene Fathers*, Series 2
ST	Thomas Aquinas, *Summa Theologica*
WSA	The Works of Saint Augustine: A Translation for the 21st Century

DOXOLOGICAL PRELUDE

Athanasius's On the Incarnation

The achievements of the Savior, effected by his incarnation, are of such a kind and number that if anyone should wish to expound them he would be like those who gaze at the expanse of the sea and wish to count its waves. For as one cannot take in all the waves with one's eyes, since those coming on elude the perception of one who tries, so also one who would comprehend all the achievements of Christ in the body is unable to take in the whole, even by reckoning them up, for those that elude his thought are more than he thinks he has grasped. Therefore it is better not to seek to speak of the whole, of which one cannot even speak of a part, but rather to recall one thing, and leave the whole for you to marvel at. For all are equally marvelous, and wherever one looks, seeing there the divinity of the Word, one is struck with exceeding awe.[1]

---

1. Athanasius, *On the Incarnation* 54 (p. 167).

Introduction

NOW AND THEN I COME ACROSS a book so good, so eye-opening, that I might have majored in the subject if I had read it early enough in my college career. And these are rarely introductory volumes. While introductions can be helpful, they tend to be so general that they really don't give me a vision of the real power and possibilities of a subject. So rather than offering only an overview of the main features of the doctrine of the atonement—something I do in the book as a whole (but not, I hope, in a manner typical of introductory volumes)—I will primarily try to take you "behind the scenes," as it were, to reflect on how one does work like this, how one comes to understand a doctrine, to conform one's mind to the patterns and shapes of a core feature of the Christian faith. Of course, the goal of theology is to delight in conforming our minds (and thus our lives) to the reality of God and his work for us and for our salvation. Theology, in short, is a work of the mind conforming itself to God's self-revelation in Jesus Christ; put differently, it is a matter of worship—of joyfully and thankfully expressing in thought, word, and deed, to God, ourselves, and others, who he is, what he has done for his creatures, and how this shapes every aspect of our lives.

So because I find methodological reflection to be dull apart from constructive development, I introduce the doctrine of the atonement by diving right in, briefly considering the role of perception or "sight" in doing theology and then unpacking the ubiquitous but rarely expounded teaching of Jesus's atonement as a work of healing.[1] For this is the God we worship: the God of our salvation, the God of our healing.

On Theologizing Well, or On "Seeing"

The challenge for students of a subject matter, including the atonement, is to learn to see things properly—and seeing is no easy task. Whereas one of us sees mere suburbia, another delights in Japanese maples, passion fruit, the occasional oriole, and different subspecies of hummingbirds in abundance. To hike in a national park with my youngest son, Simeon, is a fascinating experience: one might think the parks are uninhabited by beasts until he shows up, as his unusually keen eyes pick out mountain goats, black bears, otters, and the like. He probably spots 70 percent of the wildlife our family sees. We may or may not have functioning eyes, but seeing—seeing is an altogether different matter. As John Burroughs, an early American environmentalist, puts it: "To know is not all; it is only half. To love is the other half," for "love sharpens the eye, the ear, the touch; it quickens the feet, it steadies the hand, it arms against the wet and the cold."[2] And this sharpening of the senses by love is precisely what prepares us to see well—a point as true of theology as it is of bird watching.

In fact, we have much to learn from Burroughs's essay "The Art of Seeing Things." Sight isn't merely a matter of certain organs functioning in harmony with the physics of light; it is a matter of attention and therefore of mind or soul. For some, "their power of attention is always on the alert, not by conscious effort, but by natural habit and disposition,"[3] a disposition rooted in love. It is

1. I have had a long-standing interest in this subject, but I owe the impetus for engaging it at this particular time to a recent conversation I had with a dear friend, J. A. C. Redford, whose recent recovery from heart surgery prompted his reflection on Christ's work as healer.

2. Burroughs, *Art of Seeing Things*, 3.

3. Burroughs, *Art of Seeing Things*, 5.

precisely this disposition that allows for good seeing by fostering spontaneous and unpremeditated sight, the finding of "what you are not looking for."[4] This kind of sight seems to have two fundamental dynamics. On the one hand, there are internal forces at play: the love, knowledge, desire, and power of attention that hone our senses and prepare us to see; "the eye sees what it has the means of seeing, and its means of seeing are in proportion to the love and desire behind it. The eye is informed and sharpened by the thought."[5] On the other hand, there is something of an external nature (though still deeply internal): a war upon haste or, to put it positively, a delight in sauntering. (Psalm 1:2 may perhaps be in order here: "His delight is in the law of the LORD, and on his law he meditates day and night.") "He who runs may read some things. We may take in the general features of sky, plain, and river from the express train, but only the pedestrian, the saunterer, with eyes in his head and love in his heart, turns every leaf and peruses every line."[6] Of course, this train of thought is not at odds with the role of the mind; in fact, it delights in it. The question, rather, is a question of how the mind can step outside itself to learn, a process that begins with the heart: "You must have the bird in your heart before you can find it in the bush."[7]

And how do we translate this task of seeing in the natural environment to the work of Christian doctrine and specifically the atonement? My own approach has been to follow the logic of C. S. Lewis and to immerse myself in old books:[8] for every contemporary work I read, I read two or three ancient works. As of late, this has meant shelves full of patristic and medieval theologians: treatises, commentaries, and sermons of Augustine; many of Origen's commentaries and *On First Principles*; the writings of Maximos the Confessor,

4. Burroughs, *Art of Seeing Things*, 6.
5. Burroughs, *Art of Seeing Things*, 14.
6. Burroughs, *Art of Seeing Things*, 9–10.
7. Burroughs, *Art of Seeing Things*, 14.
8. C. S. Lewis, preface to Athanasius, *On the Incarnation*, 11–13.

Abelard, Irenaeus, Athanasius. And the key here is to saunter and to do it well, which in this case means to read whole books, to read all of Gregory the Great's *Moralia in Job* (roughly fifteen hundred pages in the translation I have) rather than simply reading the famous passages other theologians have quoted in histories of the doctrine of the atonement. The same holds, of course, for Scripture: reading small passages with great care but also reading entire books in a single sitting. To prepare for chapter 3, for instance, I took the first portion of a summer and reread the Bible cover to cover. The goal must be to see what we have not "come out to see," to find what we "are not looking for," and only the full sweep of Augustine's *On the Trinity* or the Pentateuch as a whole will do to frame those passages we want to see and, at the same time, to bring to our attention those matters we would have wanted to see, had we but known. For our goal is not to find support for what we already believe but to conform ourselves, including our minds, to a reality that exceeds us, that we might worship.

And while I have a keen eye out for works on the doctrine of the atonement, I have learned to adjust myself to ancient patterns of thought. It is easy to find the main passages where Calvin, Scheeben, or Bavinck writes about Christ's death and resurrection, but this was not always the case in theological writings, for several reasons. Partly, easy identification is due to the emergence of systematically organized works of theology (in many ways originating around the eleventh century and inspired by Peter Lombard's massively influential *Sentences*),[9] and partly it is because the atonement did not elicit controversy in the same way as did the doctrines of Christology and the Trinity, such that there are fewer works singularly devoted to the subject.

But far more importantly—most importantly—our fathers and mothers in the faith had a profound reason *not* to write single texts on Christ's work: Christ and his work are the hermeneutical key to

9. Rosemann, *Story of a Great Medieval Book*.

Scripture, the central fact giving meaning to the whole.[10] Patristic and medieval writers were nearly always thinking, to a greater or lesser extent, about the work of Christ, and they could connect the subject to nearly every passage of Scripture. For this reason, much of my reading has been in areas not specifically devoted to the subject of my research: letters, sermons, commentaries. One simply never knows when Cyril of Alexandria or Albert the Great will launch into a short but poignant exposition of the atonement. To go only to the places where one would expect the subject to be treated is to eviscerate the spirit and mindset, richly grounded in a comprehensive biblical theology, of these authors. Accordingly, my preference, where possible, is to read not merely whole works but the whole corpus of a theologian. Most of us (myself included) cannot do this with the most prolific authors (such as Augustine, Thomas Aquinas, Luther, Calvin, and Barth), but it is not difficult to read across different genres in their writings. Nor is it difficult, in the cases of many other figures, to read everything they wrote (or at least all of their works currently translated into English).

These patterns of leisurely but delighted reading, in juxtaposition with trends in contemporary works on the atonement (always, seemingly, a step behind secondary sources on the thought of particular theologians), along with regular study of the Bible, make for immensely nourishing and fruitful study of the doctrine of the atonement. They make for, in short, precisely the kind of fully engaged, delighted work of the mind that is so generative of worship. But the key, of course, is not merely to read, not merely to rush past the countryside, but to see, to truly see, to contemplate what is before us. And though reading widely may be of some help, that is not really what Burroughs has in mind.

So how does Burroughs help us to "see" the doctrine of the atonement? The key, he says, is the heart: "Nothing can take the place of love. Love is the measure of life: only so far as we love do we really

10. Young, *Construing the Cross.*

live. The variety of our interests, the width of our sympathies, the susceptibilities of our hearts—if these do not measure our lives, what does?"[11] He teaches us that the bird has to be in the heart before one can really see it: "where the art of nature is all in the direction of concealment"[12] and where the twin dangers of "petrification" and "putrefaction" endanger us, "either that we shall become hard and callous, crusted over with customs and convention till no new ray of light or of joy can reach us, or that we shall become lax and disorganized, losing our grip upon the real and vital sources of happiness and power."[13] So how do we have the doctrine of the atonement in our heart, deeply rooted in our affections, in what Plato's *Republic* (and C. S. Lewis's *Abolition of Man*, which builds upon it) would call the "spirited" part of the soul?

The key is that we have not the doctrine of the atonement in our hearts but the death and resurrection of Jesus himself. Entrance into the kingdom of God "is by practical ways, not intellectual—by following Christ; that is, by striving, with effort and prayer and self-denial, to feel with Jesus and act with Jesus and think with Jesus."[14] Each element in this statement bears consideration. Though love is nurtured by and is the impetus for the intellect, entrance into the kingdom is not primarily an intellectual matter but a practical one. It is a matter of striving, of effort. It is foremost a matter of prayer, of honoring the way that the triune God welcomes us to approach, to speak, to petition.[15] The doctrine of the atonement is built on the grounds of revelation, and it is only fitting that our methodology take up a posture conforming to the basis of its subject matter. And this prayer, while it may and should be a petition for wisdom and understanding, should likewise be an act of self-denial and repentance, an intellectual and spiritual submission, for here, as elsewhere, our sin

11. Burroughs, *Art of Seeing Things*, 4.
12. Burroughs, *Art of Seeing Things*, 8.
13. Burroughs, *Art of Seeing Things*, 4.
14. Cave, "XII," 244.
15. Cocksworth, "Prayer."

and that of our people has its shaping and perverting influence. But above all, of course, it is to take on Christ: to feel with him, act with him, and think like him—to grieve as he grieves, pray as he prays, and reflect with him on the way that the whole Old Testament bears witness to, gives shape and meaning to, the necessity of his death and resurrection.

It is as we seek to be conformed to Christ's pattern, as we have the mind of Jesus (Phil. 2:5), that we nourish and foster the kind of love that begets sight. It is the Lord who gives sight (Exod. 4:11), who gives sight to the blind (Ps. 146:8), and it is precisely this miraculous act that Jesus fulfills (Luke 4:16–21) and uses to validate his ministry to John the Baptist (Matt. 11:2–6). But the blindness in question is not merely physical (though it can include the physical); it is a matter of culpable blindness of the mind and heart (Rom. 1)—a blindness and darkness of the heart to the ways and will of God, making us liable to judgment and destruction (Isa. 56:9–12). And the recovery of this sight takes the shape of two fundamental Christian actions, both of which find their root in the work of Jesus: repentance and forgiveness. If we want to see the doctrine of the atonement, then a certain kind of love is necessary to hone, sustain, and enliven our senses. And that is a love we can have only by taking on the feelings, actions, and thoughts of Christ—acts that are impossible without repenting of our sin and forgiving the sins of others.

But what does one see when studying the work of Christ? In what follows, I try to provide an example, which we will then reflect on in a concluding methodological section.

A Particular Challenge: Unity and Diversity

The burden of the twentieth and twenty-first centuries is twofold when it comes to seeing the doctrine of the atonement: first, to continue to take up the questions and challenges that every generation of the church has had to take up and, second, to take up its own unique challenges. Those unique challenges have to do above all with the bewildering diversity emerging from critical biblical and historical work that (1) has seemed to break apart both Scripture and tradition into a cacophony of voices, (2) has placed immense pressure on groups to define themselves by claiming a single trajectory within this cacophony, and (3) has provided the church with a wealth of opportunities for new insights that have been lost or glossed over. The unique challenge of the twentieth and twenty-first centuries is thus a synthetic one: an argument for the unity proper to the diversity of the biblical witness and the history of doctrine—and with it, a suitable complexity in our account of the central aspects of the Christian faith. That is precisely the burden of this book: to explore both the abundant diversity proper to the work of Christ and the nature of its unity. It is this project of unity and diversity that will nourish the church's faith in the singular and decisive fact of the death and resurrection of Jesus for us and for our salvation—a unity that integrates the whole into a single act of understanding and worship, as well as a diversity calling for the best our minds and imaginations have to offer. And it is the love and appreciation for this unity and diversity that will, in the long run, give us the eyes to see the riches of this doctrine.

But what do I mean when I speak of a bewildering diversity? Don't views of the cross all boil down either to some form of penal substitution, in which Jesus suffers the punishment for sin in our place, or to moral exemplarism, where Jesus is the teacher or religious example par excellence (or maybe even to the ransom theory, in which Jesus defeats Satan by his death)? Not in the least. A reading of classics throughout the history of the church will quickly disabuse one of such an idea. We will explore some of this diversity in the following chapters, and I have written and edited other books on the subject.[16] Rather than retrace those lines or go further in a general account of the unity and diversity of the atonement here, we will do something

---

16. See, e.g., Johnson, *T&T Clark Companion to Atonement*; Johnson, *Atonement: A Guide for the Perplexed*.

different, something more fit to an introduction as I understand it: we will dive into one of the less developed but pervasive lines of thought in the Bible and Christian tradition—namely, that Jesus's death and resurrection was an act of healing.[17] In short, we will begin by observing, by attempting to see, one aspect of the work of Jesus Christ; from there, we will reflect on the doctrine more broadly.

By His Wounds: Atonement as Healing

The great historian of doctrine Adolf von Harnack tells of an idea that "came victoriously to the front in the Church in the third century which conceived of [redemption] as *redemption from death and therewith as elevation to the divine life, that is to say, as deification*." This "conception found a safe starting-point in the Gospel," he tells us, "but in the form in which it was now developed it was foreign [to Scripture] and conceived on Greek lines; *mortality is in itself reckoned as the greatest evil, and as the cause of all evil, while the greatest of blessings is to live forever*." He called this a "pharmacological" view, in which the "divine nature has to flow in and transform the mortal nature."[18] While Harnack dismisses the view,[19] our goal is to consider whether this ancient teaching is as sub-Christian as he thinks it is.

Descriptions of sin in terms of that which God punishes with sickness, disease, and death, as well as depictions of Christ's salvation as a work of healing, are pervasive in Scripture[20] and the history of theology. Isaiah, for instance, writes, "Surely he took up our pain and bore our suffering. . . . And by his wounds we are healed" (Isa. 53:4–5 NIV). Lanfranc of Canterbury, building upon such passages (integrating Gen. 3, Job 1–2, and Isa. 53), writes that "[Satan] inflicted punishment upon the Son of God, punishment that was to turn into

17. Bosworth, *Christ the Healer*.
18. Harnack, *What Is Christianity?*, 232–33 (emphasis original).
19. Harnack, *What Is Christianity?*, 235.
20. Reichenbach, "Healing View," 122. Cf. Deut. 28:15–28; 32:39; Pss. 41:3–8; 103:2–3; Isa. 1:5–7; 53:3–5; 57:17–19; 61:1; Hosea 5:13; 6:1–2; and Luke 4:18–19.

healing for every child of human beings."[21] But how deep does this account of healing go? Is it an image loosely connected to the work of Christ—a metaphorical gloss on deeper and more meaningful explanations—or is it a full and valid explanation of the work of Christ in its own right? In what follows, we will sketch an argument for Christ's healing atonement as a complex and thoroughgoing account of Christ's atoning work.

But what is a "complex and thoroughgoing account"? Briefly, it means that each component of the explanation follows a logic proper to the view as a whole—in this case, the categories of healing. Bonaventure, for instance, writes, "The principle of our restoration, which is Christ crucified . . . , disposes all things most wisely, being God, and heals them most mercifully, being divinity incarnate. Therefore, he ought to restore and heal the diseased human race in a manner suitable to the patient, the disease, the cause of the illness, and its cure."[22] At the very least, a satisfactory account of the atonement will include an understanding of God's character, our nature, the condition from which we suffer, the cause of this condition, and how Jesus's death and resurrection provide the cure—all in terms proper to the framework of health, disease, and cure. In this argument, I particularly focus on the writings of Augustine and Maximos the Confessor, bringing them into dialogue with a range of other theologians, demonstrating this theological elaboration of Isaiah 53:4–5 to be a rich and fully Christian Eastern-Western synthesis.[23]

---

21. Lanfranc of Canterbury, *On the Body and Blood of the Lord*, 74. Lanfranc is quoting Leo the Great, *De passione Domini* 62.

22. Bonaventure, *Breviloquium*, 212.

23. This argument, I should note, builds on the wonderful chapter by Bruce Reichenbach on the subject, which covers the biblical material related to the atonement as a work of healing. While Bruce's work is very good, it has one fundamental flaw, which I seek to remedy here by drawing on patristic and medieval theologians. Bruce makes sickness a result of guilt, thereby making atonement, as an act of healing, rest upon a foundation of moral or judicial categories pertaining to divine justice. He writes, for instance, "Of course, sin and sickness are not identical. The first is the condition, the second is the result. So we need a healer who will address both the condition and the result. Though addressing the sin is central, at the same

God as the (Incorruptible, Unchanging, and Ever-Living) Physician

Ignatius of Antioch tells us that "there is only one physician, who is both flesh and spirit, born and unborn, God in man, true life in death, both from Mary and from God, first subject to suffering and then beyond it, Jesus Christ our Lord."[24] God is the great physician, Augustine tells us.[25] According to the Psalms, "He heals the broken-hearted / and binds up their wounds" (Ps. 147:3). But while "Healer" may be a name of God, we must dig further, for as it stands, the claim is both true and unsatisfyingly negative, focused on stopping some wrong (binding a wound). Of course, as Pseudo-Dionysius teaches us, much of our naming of God is negative—proclaiming that which God is not. But can we say more? Can we name and describe God positively, praising him for who he in fact is? Who is the God who, when confronted with sickness, reveals himself as healer, as doctor? What is it of his own life and character, which he seeks to share with us, that takes the negative mode (in the sense of acting against or preventing, not in the sense of doing harm) of stanching bleeding, binding wounds, and so on?

As we look to Scripture and the history of doctrine, three candidates emerge that together form the backdrop of God's work as physician: God is incorruptible, unchanging, and living—the one who has and is life in himself. The key lies in our first quote, by Ignatius of Antioch: "There is only one physician, who is both flesh and spirit, born and unborn, God in man, true life in death, both from Mary and from God, first subject to suffering and then beyond it, Jesus Christ

---

time only by addressing the complete human condition—physical, economic, political and environmental—can we attain well-being." Reichenbach, "Healing View," 126.

In what follows, I seek to root this aspect of the atonement entirely within divine impassibility, making for a more cohesive and integrated account of atonement as healing. Sin is thus a rebellion against God's impassibility, which renders us passible. Sin does not merely result in sickness (Reichenbach, "Healing View," 129); sin is a willing entry into passibility and, therefore, sickness and death. Sin *is* sickness, a culpable sickness.

24. *To the Ephesians* 7.2, in M. Holmes, *Apostolic Fathers in English*, 98.

25. Augustine, *Expositions of the Psalms 1–32*, 230.

our Lord."[26] This claim contains four key features: (1) it names God as the physician; (2) it describes this one as having or being "true life"; (3) it depicts the movement from being "subject to suffering and then beyond it"; and (4) it grounds all of this in the person and work of Jesus Christ, in whom this movement occurs. Who is God? He is the living God who, in the person and work of Jesus Christ, moves us from subjection to suffering to a life in him that is completely beyond suffering because it is incorruptible, true life itself.

And this is the key. Who is God? Who is this God whom we might know and worship? According to one of the central insights organizing Athanasius's masterful *On the Incarnation*, God is the one who, in and of himself, is simply and purely incorruptible.[27] He is the one who is himself and has himself to such a degree and with such a finality that nothing can compromise the completeness and integrity with which he is who he is. There is no chink in the divine armor, no weak point in the supply chain that holds the economy of the triune God together—no bond or joinery within the Godhead that might be a point of weakness, tension, or conflict that could begin to break up the unity with which God is who he is. We, because we are composed of parts that can be at odds with, imbalanced in relation to, and even separated from each other; because we depend on things outside ourselves for our well-being; because we can and do choose evil paths that counter the prospering of our natures and the will of God—we are corruptible. But God—in him there are no parts, tensions, or dependencies that could result in fragmentation or conflict, leaving the door open to sickness or a fragmentation that leads to death. God, according to Athanasius, is incorruptible.

Or as Augustine puts it in his account of God as healer, whereas we are changeable (in place of Athanasius's "corruptible"), "God's essence, by which he is, has absolutely nothing changeable about its eternity or its truth or its will; there truth is eternal and love is

26. *To the Ephesians* 7.2, in M. Holmes, *Apostolic Fathers in English*, 98.
27. Athanasius, *On the Incarnation* 4–7 (pp. 59–65).

eternal; there love is true and eternity true; there eternity is lovely and truth is lovely too."[28] "Becoming a partaker of our mortality," Jesus "made us partakers of his divinity"—of his unchangeability, his eternity, of the divine life.[29] Barth, in his account of divine immutability (or divine constancy, as he prefers), writes that "as the only really living One," God's "self is neither in need of, capable of, or exposed to any annulment, decrease, increase or perversion into any other self, and His life . . . can, and does gloriously, consist only in His not ceasing to be Himself, to posit and will and perfect Himself in His being Himself."[30] Who is the God who is our healer? He is the one who in and of himself is incorruptible, changeless, constant—as the living God he is. There is no sickness nor even any preconditions that could allow for sickness in him. God is incorruptible.

Before proceeding, a brief note is in order. Much of the Christian tradition, including the patristic and medieval theologians from which I draw so heavily in this book, thinks of God as incorruptible, immutable, and impassible. This is a complex topic in its own right, in which the influence of (Platonic) philosophical presuppositions, issues of biblical interpretation, and theological commitments intersect in multifaceted ways.[31] All I can do here is try to provide a sense of the spirit motivating the use of these terms. Negatively, the goal is to reject a range of problematic views in which God is fickle, volatile, inconsistent, and in any sense "thrown about" or controlled by his creatures—all of which are deeply problematic. Positively, the spirit is one of affirming God's utter dependability, faithfulness, and

28. Augustine, *The Trinity*, 153. Pseudo-Dionysius writes that God "remains what he is—supernatural, transcendent—and he has come to join us in what we are, without himself undergoing change or confusion." In all that he is and does, God remains who he is. Pseudo-Dionysius, *Complete Works*, 66.

29. Augustine, *The Trinity*, 155.

30. Barth, *CD* II/1, 492.

31. Keating and White, *Divine Impassibility and the Mystery of Human Suffering*; Webster, "*Non ex aequo.*" While the book is about far more than these specific divine attributes, a helpful entry into the broader subject is Duby, *Jesus and the God of Classical Theism*.

constancy. God is one who, in the midst of the world's and our own chaotic changes, is who he is, remains who he is—is stable.

Sin

Against this backdrop of God's character as the incorruptible, unchanging, living one, sin emerges as a complex condition entailed by attempting to live apart from, in rebellion to, this God. Maximos writes that "the penalty imposed on the sinner is alien to Him who by nature is sinless, and this penalty is precisely the possibility of human nature as a whole."[32] This "possibility," this ability to suffer, may not seem so bad—but only at first glance. In sin, man "so drew down on himself not simply the corruption and death of his body, but also the capacity and indeed propensity for all the passions, and, not least, the instability and disorder of the material substance that surrounded him, along with its facility and susceptibility to suffer change."[33] To sin is to bring upon ourselves a state of fragmentation in which we are internally divided, vulnerable to forces inside and outside ourselves, such that we are utterly threatened by chaos and disorder. Our integrity, both physical and spiritual, is compromised, such that we are vulnerable in a host of ways, vulnerable to sickness and death. What was once whole and complete is now essentially a catastrophic and systemic collapse into suffering unto death.

Anselm, in his *Prayer to Mary* (1), writes:

> I long to come before you in my misery,
> sick with the sickness of vice,
> in pain from the wounds of crimes,
> putrid with the ulcers of sin.
> However near I am to death, I reach out to you,
> and I long to ask that by your powerful merits

32. Maximos the Confessor, *On Difficulties in the Church Fathers*, 1:23 (Ambigua 4). For an example of Maximos's account of rest and motion, see *On Difficulties in the Church Fathers*, 1:77–95 (Ambigua 7).
33. Maximos, *On Difficulties in the Church Fathers*, 1:143 (Ambigua 8).

and your loving prayers,
you will deign to heal me.[34]

Whatever you think of addressing a prayer to Mary, attend to Anselm's account of sickness, which is a collapse of integrity leading to death, a culpable sickness—that of vice—in which we are the instruments of our own demise. From this condition flows a host of wounds, ulcers, and the stench of death. Boethius, in book 1 of his *Consolation of Philosophy*, describes other aspects of this sickness, focusing on the intellectual-spiritual role of our beliefs about ourselves and our human nature. And while this is clearly a plight in which we are helplessly caught, a spiral pulling us further into ever-greater fragmentation and suffering (and finally death), we are not merely victims. Augustine describes this as a fever we suffer through our own fault.[35] Nothing about sin as sickness entails mere victimhood on the part of the patient. While illnesses and conditions exist for which we are not to blame, the picture here is a more comprehensive one. "Man had subjected himself to suffering when he transgressed the divine commandment, even though in the beginning he was impassible."[36] This is a dynamic we subject ourselves to, that we continually perpetuate, and for which we bear responsibility.

Exposing and Confessing Illness

The sickness in question is not a simple one, a wound inflicted from the outside requiring cleaning, stiches, and time to heal. It is rather a

34. Anselm, *Prayers and Meditations*, 107, lines 110–19.

35. Augustine, *Sermons (184–229z)*, Sermon 229E, pp. 282–83. Frances Young is quite incorrect in pitting healing against atonement: healing, to her, is "God's action to put things right, rather than some kind of atonement offered to God or attempt to satisfy God's demands" (Young, *Construing the Cross*, 96). The problem isn't what she affirms about healing so much as the set of dichotomies she employs, which in Scripture and the early church are held as a unity. This chapter explores the unified vision from the New Testament through, at the very least, Maximos the Confessor, whereas Young sees a rupture beginning with Augustine (*Construing the Cross*, 97).

36. Maximos, *On Difficulties in Sacred Scripture*, question 63, p. 480.

holistic condition stemming from our freely chosen departure from and rebellion against the incorruptible and ever-living God—a rebellion and willing escape from the source of our integrity, stability, and health. Our entry into healing, therefore, is necessarily a matter of exposing and confessing our condition, for the sickness stems from our will. Origen advises us, "Present yourselves to the scalpel-logos, so that the hidden things may be removed, which are stored within, and it will bring you treatment, and you may be enabled to have complete healing for your wound now, and, because you have received that complete healing, you will be made holy."[37] As Anselm puts it:

> My sins cannot be cured unless they are confessed,
>   but to acknowledge them throws me into confusion.
> If they are concealed they cannot be healed,
>   if they are seen they are detestable.
> They chafe me with sorrow, they terrify me with fear,
>   they bury me with their weight, they press upon me heavily,
>   and confound me with shame.[38]

In the words of *2 Clement*, "While we still have time to be healed, let us place ourselves in the hands of God the physician, and pay him what is due. What is that? Sincere, heartfelt repentance."[39] Augustine adds, "If only you could recognize your own sickness and be driven to seek your physician! Then you would not kill him, nor would you die of your pretended health, in your demented pride."[40] We know of stories like this: stories of friends or family members too stubborn, fearful, or proud to visit a doctor until it is too late. This, the church tells us, is precisely our condition.

And the impetus to confession is a significant one: "Nor, although he is called a physician, does he act towards all as a physician, but only

37. Origen, *Homilies on the Psalms*, 216.
38. Anselm, *Prayers and Meditations*, 109, lines 59–66.
39. *2 Clement* 9.7–8, in M. Holmes, *Apostolic Fathers in English*, 81.
40. Augustine, *Expositions of the Psalms 99–120*, Ps. 101, p. 55.

towards those who having understood their feeble and sick condition flee to his compassion that they may obtain health."[41] Were the plight merely one of victimhood, the matter might be different, but the cure is proportionate to the cause, which is, in part, a matter of free rejection of God. The cure, therefore, entails our return to him. "It is my opinion," writes Origen, "that even if someone could escape God's judgment, he ought not desire to. For not to come to God's judgment would mean not to come to correction, to the restoration of health and to that which heals."[42] The disease here is comprehensive, and so must be the cure. "It was necessary that the creator [Jesus] become obedient . . . with that obedience that would heal like medicine the disease of sin. For unless the medicine eliminated the disease, health could not emerge."[43]

On Striking and Healing, Hurting and Curing, Killing and Making Alive

Because our sickness is self-inflicted, our healing must stem from the will—a matter of volition, confession, and repentance. But this is just one aspect of our salvation. "As for us, as the logos intends, let us hear in 'I will kill and I will make alive': 'for whom will I kill but the one I would make alive, or whom would I strike but the one I would heal?'"[44] There are radical sicknesses, certain kinds of cancers and heart conditions, for which our only solution is to bring the patient as close to death as possible, to "kill" them by ending major bodily functions or removing whole organs from the body, so that we can attempt a cure and resuscitation.

To end our sickness-unto-death is not a difficult matter. God could slay us or simply allow us to live out our days in various conditions of miserable sickness-unto-death. The question, rather, is how to

41. Origen, *On First Principles*, 2:219.
42. Origen, *Commentary on the Epistle to the Romans*, 1:105.
43. William of Auvergne, *Treatise on the Reasons Why God Became Man*, 35.
44. Origen, *Homilies on the Psalms*, 348–49.

rescue a patient who must die in order to be healed, a patient whose condition is so physically, spiritually, and socially devastating that no comprehensive cure is possible apart from death.

The Unassumed Is the Unhealed

The answer, according to much of the Christian tradition, is that Jesus takes upon himself our condition, that our sickness and collapse unto death may be completed in his death, and that our healing may be made complete and final in his resurrection. The general insight here is that of Gregory of Nazianzus: "For that which He has not assumed He has not healed; but that which is united to His Godhead is also saved."[45] Augustine, for instance, writes,

> And indeed that humble doctor came, he found the patient lying sick, he shared his infirmity with him, summoning him to share his own divinity; he became in his passion the slayer of passions, and dying he was hung on the tree in order to put death to death. He made a food for us, which we were to take, and be cured. Where does this food come from? Having died, he rose again. And whom does it nourish? Those who have imitated the Lord's humility.[46]

And again, "If he in whom there was no disease submitted to the surgeon's knife, if he who is himself our healing did not refuse the searing remedy, should we be rebellious against the doctor who cauterizes and cuts, the doctor who trains us through all our troubles and heals us of our sin?"[47] Maximos makes much the same claim (particularly if we keep in mind that human passibility, the perverse ability to suffer change, was a punishment): "He also assumed the

45. Gregory of Nazianzus, "Epistle CI," 440.
46. Augustine, *Sermons (341–400)*, Sermon 341A, pp. 30–31. Cf. Augustine, *Expositions of the Psalms 33–50*, Ps. 33.2, p. 39. On sin-bearing, see Augustine, *Sermons (341–400)*, Sermon 361, p. 236.
47. Augustine, *Expositions of the Psalms 33–50*, Ps. 40, p. 231. Cf. Augustine, *Sermons (184–229z)*, Sermon 218C, p. 194.

passibility—without the sin—from the birth that was subsequently introduced into human nature. . . . It was in the possibility of Adam, on account of sin, that the wicked demons conducted their invisible operations concealed under the law of contingent human nature."[48]

Reichenbach tells of shamans who "bring about healing through the removal of the . . . cause of the illness. . . . By allegedly sucking out or removing the foreign substance or in some other way transferring the illness to themselves, shamans briefly take on the illness and suffer until they can get rid of it"[49]—an idea portrayed beautifully in Frank Darabont's adaptation of Stephen King's *The Green Mile*. This illustration gives us some traction with the idea of healing someone by absorbing their sickness into ourselves, but it is altogether too occasional, too individualistic to suffice. The church fathers had something much more fundamental in mind. The idea isn't that Jesus takes up and bears individual sicknesses and conditions in order that we might be freed from them. Rather, he takes up the human condition. Jesus takes up our possibility, our changeability. He takes up the compromised, fragmented, decaying human condition and its vulnerability—human life separated from the incorruptibility of God, life that is able to die, able to suffer, able to be torn apart both internally and externally. And he takes it up that those who are in him may have his life, his impassibility.

A Sickness Past Cure, Part 1: The Need for Death

The need for death is fundamental. This is not merely a matter of borrowing from judicial categories (e.g., penal substitution); it is an account rooted in the view of the sickness involved as well as the logic of (un)changeability and (im)passibility. Cyril of Jerusalem describes our condition as follows: "Is there no salvation henceforth? We have fallen. Is it impossible to rise again? We were blinded. Can we never recover our sight? We have become lame. . . . In a word, we are dead;

---

48. Maximos, *On Difficulties in Sacred Scripture*, question 21, p. 145.
49. Reichenbach, "Healing View," 136.

is there no resurrection? . . . He who poured out His precious blood
for us will free us from sin."[50] Justin Martyr similarly weaves together
lameness, blindness, and death in describing our condition.[51] The
condition is one so catastrophic as to necessitate death, a complete
refashioning of human existence. And while God could simply re-
create all things as an act of power, in his faithfulness he chooses to
heal us, making himself the medicine for our cure.[52] "They were kill-
ing the healer; the healer was making a medicine for his killers out of
his blood."[53] But how does this work? One of the most sophisticated
explanations I have found is that of Maximos the Confessor. Jesus

> bears the totality of human nature, including its natural, blameless
> passions, which He united to His own hypostasis. Having through
> them "consumed the meaner element"—on account of which pas-
> sibility was imposed on us in our sentence of condemnation, I mean
> *the law of sin* which arose from disobedience, whose power over us
> lies in the unnatural disposition of our will, establishing, in lesser or
> greater degrees, an impassioned state within the possible condition
> of our nature—He not only saved us who were "held captive by sin,"
> but also, by having absolved our penalty in Himself, He gave us a
> share in *divine power*, which brings about immutability of soul and
> incorruptibility of body.[54]

The eternal Son of God, through his incarnation, brought into the
divine life the human condition—the laws and patterns of the possible
human condition, which is the root of all disease, sickness, and death—
and "consumed" it within himself, in his death. Without in any way

---

50. Cyril of Jerusalem, *Works of Saint Cyril of Jerusalem*, 1:99.
51. Justin Martyr, *1 Apology* 48 (p. 56).
52. See, for instance, *Epistle of Barnabas* 8.5–6: "And then there is the matter of the wool on the piece of wood: this signifies that the kingdom of Jesus is based on the wooden cross, and that those who hope in him will live forever. But why the wool and the hyssop together? Because in his kingdom there will be dark and evil days, in which we will be saved, because the one who suffers in body is healed by means of the dark juice of the hyssop" (M. Holmes, *Apostolic Fathers in English*, 186). Cf. Bonaventure, "Tree of Life," 149–51.
53. Augustine, *Sermons (184–229z)*, Sermon 229E, p. 281.
54. Maximos, *On Difficulties in the Church Fathers*, 1:25 (Ambigua 4).

sinning or corrupting himself, Jesus "accepted their consequences, and so made birth the salvation of creaturely origin, and paradoxically renewed the incorruptibility of creation by means of the passibility made possible by his birth."[55] He "remain[ed] unconquerable in His sufferings, and appear[ed] formidable in the face of death, thereby extracting from our nature the passibility associated with pain."[56]

In himself, Jesus transforms human nature through death: he "converted the use of death, reworking it into the condemnation of sin but not of nature."[57] The account here is fundamentally representative.[58] Jesus, "whereas by nature He is impassible God, . . . deemed it worthy in His plan of salvation to become a naturally passible human being."[59] And in himself, he transforms human nature, makes a new possibility for those united to him, who submit to his healing. In him is the completion of their passibility, the "punishment of Adam's nature, and . . . 'condemn[ation of] sin in the flesh.'"[60] The resulting metamorphosis is a mystery that "brings about the utter destruction of all the properties and movements contrary to nature that were introduced into nature through the primal disobedience."[61] God became man so that by his bruises we could be healed—so that by his death our changeability and passibility, the root vulnerability to sickness and death, might be consumed.

A Sickness Past Cure, Part 2: The Need for Resurrection

This, of course, is but one half of the dynamic. Justin Martyr tells us that Christ "became man for our sakes, that, becoming a partaker of

55. Maximos, *On Difficulties in the Church Fathers*, 1:127 (Ambigua 42).
56. Maximos, *On Difficulties in Sacred Scripture*, question 21, pp. 146–47.
57. Maximos, *On Difficulties in Sacred Scripture*, question 61, p. 439; cf. 440.
58. Graham, "Substitution and Representation"; Johnson, "Barth and Boethius on *Stellvertretung* and Personhood"; Crisp, *Participation and Atonement*.
59. Maximos, *On Difficulties in Sacred Scripture*, question 54, p. 341.
60. Maximos, *On Difficulties in Sacred Scripture*, question 61, p. 439; cf. 440.
61. Maximos, *On Difficulties in Sacred Scripture*, question 63, p. 480.

our sufferings, He might also bring us healing."[62] The goal is not an end to suffering, not mere death, but healing! Augustine writes, "The Lord prayed on the mountain before his passion, and God healed him. Who was it that he healed—the Word of God, the divine Word who had never been ill? No; but he carried the death of the flesh, he carried your wound, in order to cure your wound. And his flesh was healed. When? When he rose from the dead."[63] The resurrection, on this view, is the culmination and goal of Christ's atoning act, the healing that is the whole goal of the Physician.[64] "And, just as in the beginning He brought it into being out of nothing, so too now His aim is to rescue and restore it from its fallen condition, preventing it from falling again by means of immutability, and to realize for nature the entire design of God the Father, divinizing nature by the power of His Incarnation."[65]

The resurrection is the creative, life-giving aspect of Christ's healing work, the act in which "He made our nature new, returning it to its primordial beauty of incorruptibility [and changelessness/ impassibility] through His holy flesh, taken from us, and animated by a rational soul, and on which He lavishly bestowed the gift of divinization, from which it is absolutely impossible to fall, being united to God made flesh."[66] All of the joy, goodness, and beauty of the original creative act here resounds in completion as we receive the gift of healing—of being made whole. "There is no true life but a happy life, and no true incorruption except where health has no pain to corrupt it."[67] And this is no mere resuscitation, a healing of a

62. Justin Martyr, *2 Apology* 13 (p. 84).
63. Augustine, *Expositions of the Psalms 1–32*, Ps. 29, p. 310.
64. Maximos, *On Difficulties in Sacred Scripture*, question 63, p. 492. When considering other aspects of the atonement, we will see that other moments in the life of Christ can be the culmination of the atonement as well, such as the ascension and the entry into the heavenly tabernacle. Cf. Moffitt, *Rethinking the Atonement*.
65. Maximos, *On Difficulties in Sacred Scripture*, question 54, p. 343.
66. Maximos, *On Difficulties in the Church Fathers*, 1:131 (Ambigua 42). Cf. Maximos, *On Difficulties in Sacred Scripture*, question 54, p. 352; Irenaeus, *Against Heresies* 3.18.7 (*ANF* 1:448).
67. Augustine, *Augustine Catechism*, 116.

cut or wound. This is the eschatological fruition and culmination of human nature—physical, spiritual, and social. This is the lavish gift of divinization, which Maximos unpacks partly in terms of our becoming impassible not by nature but by participation in God.[68] The resurrection "produces the perfect restoration of all the properties and movements that were previously in nature, according to which absolutely none of the principles of beings can ever be adulterated"[69]—and this last claim is key, for it follows the logic of unchangeability and incorruptibility. In Christ's resurrection, our bodies and souls are so restored to the properties and movements of human nature that no corruption, no watering down, no fragmentation, no adulteration whatsoever is possible.[70] We will be made whole. We will be awash in the divine life, living lives that are no longer capable of sickness or death, lives awash in the love and life of God.[71]

Analysis

With this reflection on Jesus as healer in mind, what have we learned about observing the doctrine of the atonement? First, we have attended to a genre of imagery that both Scripture and theologians use to describe the work of Christ, one that pertains broadly to medical or healing categories. But this, of course, is just the beginning. From there, we have drawn out the following: (1) an aspect of the character of God that gives explanatory power both to the imagery of sin (as a perversion of the character of God) and to the imagery of salvation or well-being; (2) a distinctive account of sin pertaining to that

68. Maximos, *On Difficulties in the Church Fathers*, 1:113 (Ambigua 7); Maximos, *On Difficulties in Sacred Scripture*, question 61, p. 437. Augustine makes a similar move: "Take God as your physician. Beg him to give you health and salvation, and he himself will be your salvation. Do not pray for external health merely, but for that health, that salvation, which is himself" (Augustine, *Expositions of the Psalms 73–98*, Ps. 85, p. 229).

69. Maximos, *On Difficulties in Sacred Scripture*, question 63, p. 480.

70. Maximos, *On Difficulties in the Church Fathers*, 1:25 (Ambigua 4); 1:105 (Ambigua 27).

71. Maximos, *On Difficulties in Sacred Scripture*, question 54, p. 338.

imagery, to that form of the perversion of God's character; and (3) an
account of how Jesus Christ takes upon himself the human sinful
condition in both (4) his death and (5) his resurrection so that we
can participate in the divine condition.[72] Having drawn all this out,
we can explore the full explanatory power to the imagery we first no-
ticed, moving from observation to understanding and terminating in
worship. And this, in brief, is what it means to develop a theology of
the atonement: to move from observation to understanding by integrating an explanation of how Jesus accomplishes the great exchange,
the taking of the human condition so that we can participate in the
divine life by means of his death and resurrection, in a way that fills
the biblical and homiletic imagery with meaning—or, rather, faithfully explores the power and meaning embedded in the imagery for
those with eyes to see.

An Overview of the Book

This book is not an argument for the atonement as a work of healing.
Rather, it seeks to introduce the atonement in such a way that we can
appreciate the breadth of the biblical witness to the work of Christ
and, therefore, embrace such concepts as that of Christ the healer
more fully. Such an effort requires a large-scale understanding of
the doctrine and a wide range of biblical and theological categories.
While the ultimate goal is life-changing, faithful reading of Scripture,
to get there we will be guided by some of our mothers and fathers in
the faith who have gone before us.

Chapter 1 explores the ways in which Christian theology and the
Christian reading of Scripture are ruled exercises—normed or guided
exercises. Christians, even those who believe in *sola Scriptura*, do not
read only the Bible. The Ethiopian eunuch in Acts 8:26–40 needs
someone to guide him in the *right* reading of the prophet Isaiah. One

---

72. For a slightly different and fuller account of this material in terms of five main features
of the atonement, see Johnson, *Atonement: A Guide for the Perplexed*, 47–50.

aspect of reading Scripture well (and therefore its teaching about the atoning work of Christ) is to read it in light of the creeds and confessions of the church. Chapter 1 considers how the Apostles' Creed, in particular, guides and shapes our thinking about the atonement.

Chapter 2 proceeds to give a biblical overview of the doctrine of the atonement. The goal of this chapter is to give as expansive an account as possible, allowing certain key statements in the New Testament to guide a rich retrieval of material from the Old Testament. Here, as elsewhere, the goal is not to reduce the available material so as to say, "This is the one reason why God became man." Rather, our goal is to say, "Here is yet another reason why God became man—let us add it to our list of reasons and come to know it better, that we may worship more fully."

Chapter 3 does much the same, but with the history of theology. To do so, however, we first tell a brief version of the origin of "histories of the doctrine of the atonement," together with their connection to the University of Berlin in the 1830s. With that material in place, we give an overview of the main eras in the history of the doctrine, giving an altogether different account than that developed by Gustaf Aulén in his highly influential work *Christus Victor*. As you will see, the goal here cannot be comprehensive, for the history of this doctrine is far too rich and delightfully complex to be constrained to a single chapter. My purpose, rather, is to give a sense of the overall shape of the doctrine's history and, even more important, to motivate and equip the reader to engage in some historical study (and retrieval) of their own.

Chapters 4 and 5 build on a quiet but important theme of this book. In my past works on the atonement, I have focused on the first and second articles of the Apostles' Creed. That is to say, I have mostly devoted my attention to the role of the doctrines of the Trinity, of the divine attributes, and of Christology as they relate to the atonement. In this book, I turn my attention more to the third article, considering the role of the Holy Spirit, the church, and the Christian life in relation to the work of Christ. Chapter 4 focuses on the atonement as a work of the Holy Spirit, asking how the Third Person of the Trinity plays a role in what is often developed exclusively in terms of the Father and the incarnate Son. Chapter 5 explores the relationship of the atonement to the Christian life, attending in particular to the relationship between atonement and forgiveness.

The goal of this book is not to help you stop asking questions about the atonement, resting content that you have *the* answer. Rather, its goal is to equip you with a set of biblical, theological, and historical resources so that you can ask better, harder, and more aggressive questions, having what I consider to be some of the key tools to guide you in finding those answers. May the Lord bless and keep you in your study.

DOXOLOGICAL INTERLUDE

Anselm's Meditation on Human Redemption

Christian soul, brought to life again out of the heaviness of death, redeemed and set free from wretched servitude by the blood of God, rouse yourself and remember that you are risen, realize that you have been redeemed and set free. Consider again the strength of your salvation and where it is found. Meditate upon it, delight in the contemplation of it. Shake off your lethargy and set your mind to thinking over these things. Taste the goodness of your Redeemer, be on fire with love for your Saviour. Chew the honeycomb of his words, suck their flavor which is sweeter than sap, swallow their wholesome sweetness. Chew by thinking, suck by understanding, swallow by loving and rejoicing. Be glad to chew, be thankful to suck, rejoice to swallow.[1]

1. Anselm, *Meditation on Human Redemption*, in *Prayers and Meditations*, 230.

CHAPTER ONE

The Apostles' Creed

SEEING CAN BE AS SIMPLE as attentive perception. But that is not to say that it cannot be nurtured, guided, or ruled. After all, John Burroughs wrote an essay to help us see. If our goal, for instance, is to watch vermilion flycatchers, we do well to attend to patterns having to do with geography, migration, and the like. Knowing in advance about ways of identifying calls, general aspects of bird anatomy, relative groupings based on the size or shape of tails, whether the birds walk or hop when on land, and so on forms a set of tools for honing our perception of the birds we see, making all the difference when it comes to identifying a particular bird. The same is true of any kind of seeing, including theological seeing. This chapter offers a sketch of some of the ways in which ruled Christian thinking[1]—thought guided by authority, particularly by creeds and confessions (in this case, the Apostles' Creed)—both constrains and equips our perception and understanding of Christ's atoning work.

This may seem to be an odd decision, given the obvious fact that the Apostles' Creed rests content with an economical narration of

1. Cf. Webster, *Confessing God*, 29, 69–83.

31

Jesus's incarnation, death, and resurrection—no account of defeating death, of removing sin, of how these events are effective for us, of how they change us and our relationship to God.[2] The Apostles' Creed simply doesn't advance a "theory" of the atonement. But that is not a problem; we are looking to the creed not so much to find a theology of the atonement as to find a guide for it, to provide the rhyme and the meter within which the poetry takes shape. It might be tempting to think that the guidance comes from the "second article" alone— the portion of the creed pertaining to Jesus—but this is not the case at all. Christian thinking forms a whole, in which every part shapes our understanding of the whole and vice versa.

In what follows, we move through the Apostles' Creed point by point, attending to some of the ways in which certain aspects of the creed—we don't have the space for a full account—play a particularly important role in properly perceiving and understanding the saving work of Christ. For the Christian faith as a whole, both in the form of a creed and in a more expansive version, guides and shapes worship—in this case, worship of what God has done for us in Jesus Christ.

In exploring the relationship between the atonement and the core of the Christian faith, we have room but for the briefest gesture toward relevant sources on the subject. To give some coherence to this section, I will particularly emphasize the following four works: Augustine's *Enchiridion*, Thomas Aquinas's *Sermon-Conferences on the Apostles' Creed*, Calvin's *Institutes*, and Barth's *Dogmatics in Outline*.

"I Believe"

The doctrine of the atonement falls within the sphere of belief, of faith. We access the cross, the resurrection, and their meaning as

---

2. "It is one of the more remarkable and remarked upon aspects of theological history that no theory of atonement has ever been universally accepted. By now, this phenomenon is itself among the things that a proposed theory of atonement must explain." Jenson, *Systematic Theology*, 1:186.

an act of faith, of responding to God's self-revelation in Scripture, a revelation of his interpretation of these events. The Christian life consists of the human faculties conforming to the reality of God and his kingdom; the doctrine of the atonement is the fruit of the mind delighting in the God-given revelation that the death and resurrection of Jesus are the work of God to reconcile all things to himself. The doctrine speaks of a peace that "surpasses all understanding, and we can only know it by coming to it."[3] Though the mind cannot but use the tools and resources it inherits from the people(s) and culture(s) that nourish and guide it, doctrine remains an act of a faithful mind. Belief in Christ's atonement is an act of faith.

The doctrine of the atonement, therefore, is not a matter of natural theology or of apologetics; it is not a matter of cultural plausibility structures, of proving the historicity of the resurrection, or of demonstrating that Christian commitments do or do not comport with certain contemporary or historical legal or penal sensibilities. Such efforts may have a role to play; proving that the atonement was necessary or likely to happen apart from scriptural revelation may be a valid enterprise. (I have my doubts.) But the fundamental task is that of properly, faithfully, responding to "*the self-presentation of the triune God, the free work of sovereign mercy in which God wills, establishes and perfects saving fellowship with himself in which humankind comes to know, love and fear him above all things.*"[4] The burden of the doctrine of the atonement is not to conform to our sensibilities but to fit, mold, and shape those sensibilities to the truth. Accordingly, it is an act of hubris, of sin, to base Christian doctrine on our cultural sensibilities. We do not work in a vacuum, completely separate from culture; theology, too, is a human enterprise, subject to all its weaknesses or threats. But doing Christian doctrine, as with "reading Holy Scripture," involves

3. Augustine, *Augustine Catechism*, 91.
4. Webster, *Holy Scripture*, 13 (emphasis original); cf. 16–17.

"'faithful' reading: exegetical reason caught up in faith's abandonment of itself to the power of the divine Word to slay and to make alive."[5] Here, as elsewhere, "the definitive act of the church is faithful hearing of the gospel of salvation announced by the risen Christ in the Spirit's power through the service of Holy Scripture. As the *creatura verbi divini*, the creature of the divine Word, the church is the hearing church."[6] As the Ten Theses of Bern (1528) affirm, "the holy, Christian Church, whose only Head is Christ, is born of the Word of God, abides in the same, and does not listen to the voice of a stranger."[7]

Perhaps Anselm's language of satisfaction was derived from his feudalistic context;[8] our modern views of the penitentiary system may or may not allow for the death penalty; and current psychological studies may think of guilt or shame as good or bad, as real or as social constructs. We can, of course, only think and speak with the conceptual tools of our culture. We do not make up words, categories, or modes of logic ex nihilo; they come from the cultural inheritance we receive from the communities that raise us. Theology is a human task. But its validity hinges on the belief, on the conformity of the mind to the fact, that the risen Lord confronts his church, that he is the basis by which culture and its tools are judged or, more fruitfully, brought into service of a reality greater than themselves, brought into the service of the maker and remaker of heaven and earth.

The doctrine of the atonement is an act of faith—of faith seeking understanding rooted in the self-revelation of God. It is a work in which our minds, along with our language and presuppositions, conform to a reality greater than a merely historical, social, or cultural one.

5. Webster, *Holy Scripture*, 86–87. Cf. Gregory of Nazianzus, *On God and Christ*, 89; Barth, *Dogmatics in Outline*, 23.
6. Webster, *Holy Scripture*, 44.
7. Cochrane, *Reformed Confessions of the 16th Century*, 49.
8. Southern, *Saint Anselm and His Biographer*, 107–14.

"God, the Father Almighty"

The atonement revolves around the death and resurrection of Jesus of Nazareth, but "all . . . Christian doctrines [including the atonement] are applications or corollaries of the one doctrine, the doctrine of the Trinity."[9] The death and resurrection of Jesus have meaning—they shape all of reality—because Jesus has a Father. (On the role of the Holy Spirit, see chap. 4.) The work of Jesus is a work of obedience—of saying yes to, of following the will of, another, whom he calls "Father." The creed begins not with Jesus but with the one who stands behind the work of Jesus, who wills and plans it, who asks it of his Son.[10] It is the purpose of the Father, the delight and anger of the Father, that provides the fundamental shape of the pattern and history into which Jesus enters as the Messiah of God's chosen people.[11] To ignore the Father is to ignore the whole background of God's covenantal history with Israel: God's plan to judge and to reverse the consequences of the fall through Abraham, Isaac, Jacob, and their offspring and to bring about a salvation that has the contour and shape God planned from the beginning.

To dwell on the Father's work of atonement is to conform to the trinitarian shape of the doctrine—that this is the one work of the one God, willed by the Father, Son, and Holy Spirit.[12] The atonement is the fruit, the enactment of the unity, of the one God, flowing from his proper and constitutive unity, enveloping us in our fragmentation, and inviting us into unity in him (John 17). The atonement is about the problem of sin, but even more so, it is about the problem of fulfilling God's creative purposes for a fallen creation, not merely overcoming his wrath or anger. The root of the atonement is the Father's love (though a proper understanding of how God relates to sin is a further and necessary understanding of this point).

9. Webster, *Holy Scripture*, 43.
10. Barth, *CD* IV/1, 4.
11. Cyril of Alexandria, *Glaphyra on the Pentateuch*, 1:156.
12. Johnson, *Atonement: A Guide for the Perplexed*, 59–88.

But the creed invites us to think of the Father's might, as twice he is named as "almighty." The atonement is a work of God's power, as the hinge between creation and eschatology, which are likewise works of his power. Here, we take up our earlier point that the doctrine of the atonement is a work of faith—here, as elsewhere, we must learn about power from God's self-revelation, not from any other source.[13] God's power is his ability to fashion creation, to call it into being—but also his power is to enter creation, to take it upon himself, to become a creature, and to make the creature like himself. But more than the power to become a creature, the atonement is the power of God's justice, the power of law,[14] and therefore the power of goodness— the power to transform creation,[15] bringing it to his right hand in heaven. Jesus is God's power to be faithful to both himself and his creation, not only the absolute power of creation out of nothing, not merely the active power of saving, but the power to be faithful to, to make covenant with, to be just toward, to transform from within by participating in and suffering with his creation.[16]

"Creator of Heaven and Earth"

Heaven and earth compose the totality of existence other than God himself, the existence God brought into being in his power and joy. And according to Scripture, it is this reality of heaven and earth that sets the stage for the doctrine of the atonement (rather than a narrower focus on sin or anthropology). Of course, the burden of sin rests heavy upon us, and our guilt cries out to God. But our

13. See the implicit account of God's power in, for instance, Webster, *God without Measure*, 1:101–8.

14. Barth, *Dogmatics in Outline*, 48.

15. Augustine, *The Trinity*, 356.

16. See, for instance, the thorough integration of justice and power (not to mention goodness, wisdom, and love) in the patristic question of why God didn't simply overpower Satan. Cf. Augustine, *The Trinity*, 355–60. Patristic discussions about Christ's defeat of Satan are fundamentally about the relationship between divine power and divine justice as well as the inseparability of the two.

Lord is the maker of heaven and earth, not merely the God of Israel and the head of his body, the church. True, as Calvin puts it, "by his love God the Father goes before and anticipates our reconciliation in Christ. Indeed, 'because he first loved us' [1 John 4:19], he afterward reconciles us to himself." But this love is grounded in the "love with which God embraced us 'before the creation of the world,'" which "was established and grounded in Christ [Eph. 1:4–5]," by whom all things were created (Col. 1:16).[17] The problem consists of a whole set of dualities (not dichotomies) for which the death and resurrection of Jesus is the solution.

It is not clear, for instance, whether physical or spiritual ailment is preeminent in the eyes of the Creator. Sometimes Jesus forgives and then heals as a sign of his authority; other times he simply heals and then tells the person to sin no more. The sign of his messianic status is his work of healing. Behind this physical-spiritual duality stands a second duality, which we might call the natural-supernatural. Did God become man to reconcile us to himself (an anthropological emphasis), or did he become man to bring order to the spiritual-heavenly realm, overthrowing Satan? Scripture knows of no dichotomy, though it embraces the duality—the atonement is God's work to reconcile the whole of God's creation to himself, ourselves included.

Broadly put, creation is the God-elected and God-created context for enacting his power and taking up responsibility—the responsibility of bringing creation to fulfillment, of recapitulating his creative work in the re-creative work of the incarnate Son.[18] "The Incarnation," Bonaventure tells us, "is the work of the First Principle, not only insofar as it is an effective principle in producing, but also insofar as it is a restorative principle in healing, atoning, and reconciling."[19] Recent years have seen a growing interest in the idea of the atonement

17. Calvin, *Institutes* II.xvi.4 (p. 506).
18. This is one of the fundamental insights of Irenaeus and of Athanasius's great work, which follows in his footsteps, though it also pervades patristic and medieval theology, such as Anselm's account of honor. Cf. Athanasius, *On the Incarnation* 4–7 (pp. 59–65).
19. Bonaventure, *Breviloquium*, 136.

as God's act of repentance or penance for this sinful and fallen world into which we are born.[20] This is but a parody of the gospel and the true nature of the responsibility God embraces for creation—the freedom and constancy with which he not only creates but accompanies his creation; with which he is free to be responsible, while granting his creatures freedom and inviting them into responsibility; and with which a greater form of responsibility exists than that stemming from guilt. It is a responsibility rooted in the unique and faithful power of God: his freedom and ability to take responsibility for fallen creation, bringing it to the completion of a full and joyful responsibility in him.

"I Believe in Jesus Christ, His Only Son, Our Lord, Who Was Conceived by the Holy Spirit and Born of the Virgin Mary"

We come now to the second article of the creed—the affirmation of belief in Jesus Christ, the Son of God the Father. This man is the revelation of the Father, his perfect image, his Word, and therefore his Word to us. The doctrine of the atonement revolves around the events of this man's life—not merely in certain beliefs, philosophies, or ideas. The creed tells us that this one who is the Son of God (1) is Lord, (2) was conceived by the Holy Spirit, and (3) was born of the Virgin Mary. That Jesus is Lord locates the creed, a theological statement, at least in part as a political statement, which we will explore in the next section.[21]

This Lord is conceived by the Holy Spirit and born of the Virgin Mary. In him is the whole being, character, and perfection of God, for he is fully God. This is the one by whom and in whom the Father created all things, the one in whom all things hold together (Col. 1:17). This is the perfect revelation of God, for he is God. This is the form the life and responsibility of God take in relation to his creation,

20. Adams, *Christ and Horrors*, 242–81.
21. Augustine, *The Trinity*, 367n336.

for he is the good Lord of his creatures. We will attend to the role of the Holy Spirit within the atonement in chapter 4. For now, we consider that Jesus was born of the Virgin Mary: he is fully man, the one who makes known to us what it is to be human, for in him is the long-lost archetype, the uncorrupted picture, the uncorrupted model, and the ultimate telos for our kind.[22] This one, this Lord, is fully God and fully man, the mediator, the one who in himself and his history lives simultaneously the history of God and the history of humankind.

But what of Mary? What can we say of her in relation to Christ's atoning work? Blessed is she among women, to be sure (Luke 1:42). But can we say more? Can we, ought we, go so far as to say something substantive about her work in our redemption? Anselm prays to Mary:

> By you the elements are renewed, hell is redeemed,
> demons are trampled down and men are saved,
> even the fallen angels are restored to their place.[23]

Caravaggio, in his *Madonna and Child with St. Anne*, portrays Mary teaching her young son how to crush the head of the serpent. Others have spoken of her as co-redemptrix or co-mediatrix.[24] So far, I have been able to recognize only her faithful passivity, to affirm that her activity is that of availing herself to be the material cause of our salvation, the one in and by whom the Lord took on the flesh of Israel so as to become its Messiah, thereby blessing the nations.[25] Further than

22. As R. S. Peterson puts it, "The teleological dimension of being made in God's image is the identifying characteristic of this particular creature that sets the context for all other aspects of theological anthropology." Peterson, *The* Imago Dei *as Human Identity*, 69.

23. Anselm, *Prayers and Meditations*, 119–20, lines 154–56. To be fair to Anselm, though, he consistently speaks of Mary in his three prayers to her as the material, not the efficient, formal or final cause of our salvation.

24. Hauke, *Introduction to Mariology*, 307–36.

25. As Ables puts it, "Of course, Mary is the agent of salvation insofar as she is the mother of Christ; salvation occurs through her, that is, because she is the bearer of the incarnation." Ables, *Body of the Cross*, 83.

this I cannot go for fear of adding layers of seemingly pious mediation between ourselves and our Lord—layers that, in effect, create a
greater distance between ourselves and the one who draws near to
us, the mediator who is both God and man.

"He Suffered under Pontius Pilate"

The creed's jump from the incarnation to its testimony that Jesus
suffered under Pilate raises two questions: (1) What of Jesus's life
as a whole? And (2) why the emphasis on suffering? Calvin tells
us that whereas the whole life of Jesus is saving, the creed leaps to
the death of Christ.[26] But how is Jesus's life saving? Several answers
come to mind. First, Jesus's life provides us the necessary revelation
of God and, simultaneously, the equally necessary human example
and model for the Christian life, essential aspects of our salvation,
in which God resolutely determined not merely to exercise his pure
and undiluted power to accomplish his ends but to exercise his
good and faithful power to save us as the creatures we are—and
therefore as creatures who learn and become who they are by mod-
els, images, patterns, and habits, all of which call for an exemplar.[27]
The Christian life is one of abiding in Jesus, of taking up our cross
and following him, of Christlikeness. God did not dispense with
his creatures, nor did he simply start anew. As Athanasius tells it,
God repainted his image on us, his tarnished and damaged image
bearers.[28]

Second, Jesus's whole life is saving in that it is, as Irenaeus teaches
us, recapitulating.[29] God delights in the relative and delegated power
he gives to his creatures—power that is real and remains (albeit in
diminished and perverse form) even in rebellion against its source.
But the power of God (and therefore our own power) is the power

---

26. Calvin, *Institutes* II.xvi.5 (p. 507).
27. Thomas Aquinas, *ST* III.46.43–44.
28. Athanasius, *On the Incarnation* 13–14 (pp. 77–81).
29. Hart, "Irenaeus, Recapitulation and Physical Redemption."

to be faithful to others, to make covenants. His power being such, God delights in preserving and being faithful to the covenants and histories of his creatures: faithful to the history of Adam and his people and, more particularly, Abraham and his people; faithful to his promises to them and to their promises to other nations; and faithful even to Satan and the limited power he gave him to be the prince of the power of the air (Eph. 2:2). God is a God who, in and through his power, is and remains faithful.

For this reason, God is a God who recapitulates, who takes up the myriad threads of the purposes, promises, and details of his history with his people, fulfilling them in himself. Jesus, like his people, is born of promise. He, like his people, flees into Egypt to grow strong. He, like his people, is baptized, entering into his promised land. He, like Moses, ascends a mountain to give his people the law. And this is where the Old and New Testaments leap to life, for Jesus is not merely a new version of the old. He is the eternal, heavenly pattern on which the old was built, and he enters creation as its fulfillment. He is the true temple, who fulfills both the history and telos of the old temple.[30] The same can be true of the law or the role of the Spirit, of every key element in the history of Israel. Why the life of Christ? Because God is not merely powerful to save; he is faithful—and therefore faithful to save in a way that honors and fulfills not only a product but a whole history and calling.

But why did he suffer? The Christian witness is that God became man in order to suffer—not *only* to suffer but *also* to suffer. The purpose of Christology is to be able to affirm both *that* God suffered and *how* God suffered—by means of his manhood, by means of his flesh.[31] But the goal, the purpose, was that he might suffer, not in a final and ultimate sense but in fulfillment of creation's fallen state— its movement unto death under the curse, under its opposition to its maker. God became man in order to suffer, in order to "shoulder

30. Beale, *The Temple and the Church's Mission*.
31. Gavrilyuk, "God's Impassible Suffering in the Flesh."

the full punishment of sin, and so expiate all of its guilt"—a reality as encompassing of the soul as it is of the body.[32]

And Christ suffered under Pontius Pilate. The American people talk of a "separation of church and state," but the Apostles' Creed knows of no such dichotomy. Jesus is Lord; the relegation of Christian faith to a private or religious sphere is as nonsensical as the notion of a private or personal president or country. This one, who is the Son of God, suffers under the lord of this age and under the representative of Caesar, Pontius Pilate—the one who holds the power to free or to crucify (John 19:10). But over and against this power stands a greater power, a greater lordship that grants this provisional power to Pilate and Caesar.[33] This is a matter between "God's kingdom and the *polis*," for "world-history so far as at all times . . . is ordered on State lines."[34] Here is the authority behind creation: the creator of natures, the giver of laws, the bestower of power and responsibility, the judge. And we are to repent of the ways in which our cultures, the nations in which we live and of which we are a part, permeate our souls, our bones— the ways in which we, too, are men and women of unclean lips (Isa. 6:5). Jesus's death and resurrection are the judgment of the political powers of this world and the establishment of his eternal kingdom.

"Was Crucified, Died, and Was Buried"

Why was Jesus crucified? The answer is complex, and our temptation is to reduce this complexity, to artificially simplify it, for reasons benign or not so benign in service of our own ideologies or purposes. Just as the medieval theologians delighted in using Aristotle's four causes (material, efficient, formal, and final),[35] we will do the same in answering our question, in a gesture at the complexity of this event.

---

32. Thomas Aquinas, *Sermon-Conferences on the Apostles' Creed*, 79.

33. Calvin, *Institutes* II.xvi.5 (pp. 508–9).

34. Barth, *Dogmatics in Outline*, 110.

35. Briefly, a *material cause* is what a thing is made of (its material), an *efficient cause* is what it was made by (a tool), a *formal cause* is the form or idea of the thing that is made (a pattern or blueprint, we might say), and a *final cause* is the ultimate goal for which a thing is made.

Materially, Jesus was crucified because he had a body of good integrity, and it was hung from wood with nails. A normal body nailed to a cross is a crucified body. That may not seem like much of an answer, but it is a part of a full account.

When it comes to the efficient cause of his death, things get a little more complicated. I can discern at least five efficient causes. First, Satan was an efficient cause of Jesus's crucifixion. After Jesus's temptation in the desert, Luke tells us that the devil "departed from him until an opportune time" (Luke 4:13). There is every reason to think, in light of the shape of Jesus's struggle with demons and Satan, that the cross is Satan's final temptation. (The parallel of Satan's intensifying oppressions of Job is vital here.) Second, Scripture likewise indicates that Judas handed over or betrayed Jesus to be crucified, partly through Satan's leading (Luke 22:3). Third, Judas did not act alone, for he collaborated with the chief priests (Matt. 26:14), who, fourth, themselves handed Jesus over to the Romans, the ones who finally crucified Jesus—but only against their will. Scripture, in other words, portrays a whole host of efficient causes, of active moral agents seeking and bringing about the crucifixion of Jesus. But, fifth, behind all these causes stands the will of the triune God—"the will of the LORD to crush him" (Isa. 53:10).[36]

. And what of the formal cause, the idea that gives shape to the action? Here, too, we have a conjunction of causes. On the Jewish side, we have the belief that "if a man has committed a crime punishable by death and he is put to death, and you hang him on a tree, his body shall not remain all night on the tree, but you shall bury him the same day, for a hanged man is cursed by God" (Deut. 21:22–23). Along with that was the understanding that those crucified were exposed to the demonic, the rulers of the air. On the Roman side was the belief that suspension in the air by a tree (it need not be "cross-shaped") was an act that heaped shame upon the victim, exposing their weakness

36. Webster, "'It Was the Will of the Lord to Bruise Him.'" On the suffering servant in Isaiah, cf. Janowski and Stuhlmacher, *Suffering Servant*; Bellinger and Farmer, *Jesus and the Suffering Servant*.

before the power of Rome—a clear and brutal social and political statement. Why was Jesus crucified? That he might be cursed, exposed, and shamed by Satan, Israel, and Rome. Curse and shame, we might say, are the formal causes of the crucifixion.

Beyond that, we should speak of two other formal causes. The first pertains to the two trees in the garden of Eden (i.e., the tree of life and that of the knowledge of good and evil). In the two beams of the cross, we have represented both of those trees: the tree that, through sin, brings death and ignorance and the tree that, through Jesus's saving work, brings life and knowledge. In this sense, the formal cause of the crucifixion is the archetypal reality of Eden, which Christ recapitulates. Second, the church fathers speak of the crucifixion as a death in which Jesus stretched out his arms to the left and the right to draw the Jews and the gentiles to himself.[37] The formal cause of the crucifixion would, in this sense, be reconciliation.

The final cause of the crucifixion is, as with all things, the glory of the Lord. Jesus, before his crucifixion, prays: "Father, the hour has come; glorify your Son that the Son may glorify you" (John 17:1). The question is this: In what sense does the cross glorify the Father? The answer here is twofold. First, we must anticipate a point we will shortly make in more depth: strictly speaking, the cross itself does not glorify the Father. It is too negative an act to glorify the Father in a sufficiently clear manner. It is good, it is necessary, and it is glorious— but only the unremitting joy and creative power of the resurrection are fully worthy, fully fitting to glorify the Father. Second, the crucifixion glorifies the Father in a secondary, qualified, and negative way by bringing to completion God's rejection of and judgment upon sin: "It had to happen in this way in order that the whole curse—which on account of our sin awaited us, or rather lay upon us—might be lifted from us, while it was transferred to him."[38] Scripture is replete with witnesses to the judgment of God, his wrath, the destructiveness

37. Athanasius, *On the Incarnation* 25 (p. 105); Thomas Aquinas, *ST* III.46.44.
38. Calvin, *Institutes* II.xvi.6 (p. 510).

of his holiness and righteousness—in short, the witness that for God to approach and be near to sin, to his sinful and rebellious creation, is for him to judge, destroy, and do away with it. From the threat of death in Genesis (Gen. 2:17) to the threats of judgment in Deuteronomy (Deut. 28:15–68) and the eschatological vision of judgment in the book of Revelation, to stand opposed to God, unreconciled to him, is to suffer his judgment and wrath. The final cause of the cross, negatively understood, is the glorious revelation and enactment of God's opposition to his sinful creation.

It was for this reason that Jesus came: to die, to sum up in himself the curse upon creation, crushing, breaking, and scattering its whole force.[39] Or put positively, it was to sum up in himself God's faithfulness to himself, a faithfulness to his holiness and justice so complete and pure that nothing but death and rejection is fitting for anything to the contrary. It was the will of the triune God to be faithful to himself and to creation's fallenness in himself, in Jesus Christ. And the culmination of this act, of dying, is burial—a recapitulation of the history of humankind in returning to the dust whence we came (Gen. 3:19). The flood was but a partial return to the formless void of precreation. Jesus's death is the fulfillment of that same impetus: the decreation of life, of all creation in Christ, in his return to the dust.

Are all these answers too poetic, one might ask? The answer here must be brief. The God of creation is a poetic God, creating in a poetic structure. One need only look at the language in Genesis 1:1–2:3 (not to mention the entire book of Psalms) to see that God is poetic. That being the case, our logic, our theology, must likewise be poetic, sensitive to pattern, symmetry, and a musical sense of the unfolding and fulfilling of theme and countertheme.[40] Anything less will simply fail to capture the patterns of thought God reveals to be his own.

39. Calvin, *Institutes* II.xvi.6 (p. 511).
40. Hogg, *Anselm of Canterbury*.

"He Descended to Hell"

It ought first be said that Christ's descent into hell is a contested feature of the Apostles' Creed, added relatively late in its history.[41] For the sake of this book, however, I will assume the legitimacy of its inclusion,[42] and in keeping with the emphasis in this book of introducing theology via particulars rather than by general introduction, we will dive into this particular point in a little more depth. There are two fundamental interpretative possibilities for understanding Christ's descent: (1) the harrowing of hell states that Jesus entered the underworld as a victor, there to liberate the captives who, while faithful to God and his promises, were nonetheless awaiting God's work in Christ to deliver them from the power of sin, death, and the devil. The impetus here is a fundamentally victorious one, a triumphant raid and decisive overthrowing of that which had been an indomitable power, an imperturbable kingdom.[43] Since most theologians who affirm the descent do not contest this point, and since it is reconcilable with the second interpretation (as a two-step process), we will devote our attention to the second interpretation: (2) that Christ descended into hell at least partly in order to "suffer the full punishment of sin, and so expiate its guilt. The punishment of sin for humanity, however, was not only the death of the body, but also involved the soul, because sin also belonged to the soul."[44]

The general consensus is that Jesus came to suffer, but did he come to suffer death or the experience of being dead?[45] "If Christ had died only a bodily death," Calvin writes (in keeping with the logic of Thomas Aquinas), "it would have been ineffectual."[46] In other words, was the triune God's negative purpose that Jesus die (a

---

41. Schaff, *Creeds of Christendom*, 1:19.
42. Cf. Calvin, *Institutes* II.xvi.8 (p. 513).
43. Emerson, *"He Descended to the Dead."*
44. Thomas Aquinas, *Sermon-Conferences on the Apostles' Creed*, 79.
45. Lauber, *Barth on the Descent into Hell*.
46. Calvin, *Institutes* II.xvi.10 (p. 515). Cf. Thomas Aquinas, *Sermon-Conferences on the Apostles' Creed*, 79–85.

work accomplished on Good Friday) or the more radical purpose of him experiencing what those dead in their sin undergo (a work accomplished on Holy Saturday)? Did Jesus suffer the reality of hell in some meaningful sense, or did he simply enter hell, unperturbed by its darkness, much like the angel in Dante's *Divine Comedy* before the city of Dis?[47]

The challenge is to unpack the reality of the curse that Christ came to bear.[48] Was it merely the curse of death ("When you eat from it you will certainly die" [Gen. 2:17 NIV]), or was the curse more comprehensive than that? Did the curse entail the full reality of hell, as taught throughout the New Testament? If so, then the logic of the great exchange, that Jesus came to bear what is ours so that we might have what is his, seems to entail that Jesus would in some way take upon himself our hell, as we (like Milton's Satan) bear our own hell with us. One of the main questions here is whether the Son of God (even in his incarnate state) *can* experience hell. After all, Thomas writes that Jesus had an unperturbed beatific vision of the Father.[49]

Barth and Balthasar[50] offer particularly constructive developments of the doctrine of Christ's descent into hell, while many argue against it, most recently Matthew Emerson.[51] An argument I would like to add to these considerations is a biblical one. In short, the Bible demonstrates a pervasive pattern of God working through or by means of the experience of the suffering of death (not merely of dying but of an active suffering of death itself)—a pattern that Jesus fulfills in a greater and more perfect way. Recall the logic of Hebrews: in the past, the priest would enter the earthly tabernacle with the blood of goats to make purification, but now our great high priest has entered the heavenly tabernacle, offering his own more perfect blood. The logic is not merely that a "greater than" has occurred, but that the

47. Dante, *Inferno* 9.75–105, pp. 91–93.
48. Calvin, *Institutes* II.xvi.10–12 (pp. 515–20). Cf. Barth, *Dogmatics in Outline*, 118–20.
49. Thomas Aquinas, *ST* III.46.47.
50. Lauber, *Barth on the Descent into Hell*; Oakes, "Internal Logic of Holy Saturday."
51. Emerson, *"He Descended to the Dead."*

perfect, heavenly reality has come among us and fulfilled its own proper dynamic in a manner hinted at by signs and shadows. This, I suggest, is precisely what we see writ large across the Old Testament.

Joseph is nearly killed by his brothers (they tell his father he has been killed), is sold into slavery, and then finds himself in prison for a crime of which he is innocent. But attend to the imagery: the brothers nearly kill him, they give evidence of his having been killed, and he ends up in prison—an image for the underworld. But in his suffering, God is with him and blesses both the people of Israel and the Egyptians in the process. This, of course, is but the establishment of a pattern to be fulfilled on a larger scale. Israel itself descends into Egypt to escape death and ends up in bondage and captivity—a form of prison, recapitulating the story of Joseph. But in their suffering, in this house of death, God comes to them and blesses them (and through them, in the long run, Egypt). The pattern continues: Samson, in his folly, betrays himself to Delilah and is blinded and imprisoned (both darkness and prison being images for the underworld). And God answers his prayer—he uses Samson, in his suffering, one last time to deliver the Israelites from their oppressors.

We find the same pattern in the stories of Job, Daniel, Daniel's three friends, and Jonah. God allows Job to be tested by Satan in a host of ways—and only in and through the immense suffering of Job, a suffering akin to death, does God use him to triumph over Satan, and he subsequently blesses Job mightily. Daniel is lowered into the pit, surrounded by lions—but God blesses him in this place of death. Much the same happens to Shadrach, Meshach, and Abednego, who are faithful even in the furnace. Jonah paints a slightly different kind of picture.[52] The rebellious prophet has himself cast into the sea, sinks down to the place of the dead, is swallowed by a monster of the deep (all images of death and the afterlife), and remains inside it for three days and three nights (the sign of Jonah [Matt. 12:38–42]). From the belly of the fish, he prays:

52. McLay, *Use of the Septuagint in New Testament Research*, 159–69.

> In my distress I called to the LORD,
>> and he answered me.
> From deep in the realm of the dead I called for help,
>> and you listened to my cry.
> You hurled me into the depths,
> ....
> I said, "I have been banished
>> from your sight;
> yet I will look again
>> toward your holy temple."
> ....
> To the roots of the mountains I sank down;
>> the earth beneath barred me in forever.
> But you, LORD my God,
>> brought my life up from the pit. (Jon. 2:2–4, 6 NIV)

Two points are particularly worth noticing in this prayer. First, imagery pertaining to the underworld fills the prayer: references to being barred in forever, to the pit, to being banished from God's sight, to being cast into the sea. Second, this prayer comes from a place of suffering. The experience is one of banishment, distress, and tears. Jonah cries out to the Lord for help. He is surrounded, threatened, dragged down, and his life is ebbing away. There is a longing for, an anticipation of, salvation from the Lord. The fact that the prayer is to God, that it is a faithful and therefore ultimately hopeful prayer, does nothing to mitigate that this is also a prayer of suffering from the underworld.

Is this scriptural pattern conclusive? Does it prove that Jesus suffered in hell? No, it does not. But just as Jesus's was a greater sacrifice than those offered in the Old Testament, just as he is a greater king, the giver of a greater law, and so forth, is he not a greater sufferer? Does he not fulfill that which the Old Testament could only hint at? Is he not the archetype of Joseph, Job, and others, recapitulating their experiences in his own life, particularly in his descent into hell? Over and over again, God reveals himself to be one who brings his servants, or allows them to be brought, into conditions of intense suffering, which only the language of death, Sheol, and (in New Testament terms) hell can adequately describe. And in this suffering, he reveals himself to be the one who hears the cry of his people, who saves them out of prison, out of captivity, out of the pit, the cave, the belly of the fish—out of suffering and godforsakenness and hell.

When we combine (1) this repeated pattern, (2) the logic of Hebrews that God has come among us as the perfect fulfillment of these shadowy anticipations, and (3) the point that God became man to take upon himself our curse (Gal. 3:13)—the reality and consequences of our sin—I find it deeply and richly compelling not only that Jesus died for us and for our salvation but that he descended into hell for us, that he experienced the fundamental curse from which we need to be, we long to be, delivered.[53]

"On the Third Day He Rose Again from the Dead"

I had been a Christian for a long time before I understood that the resurrection mattered for the Christian life. I believed it to be true. I had read a book arguing for the historicity of the resurrection. But I just didn't understand how or why it mattered. Two sources revolutionized my thinking on the subject. First, I read T. F. Torrance's *Space, Time, and Resurrection*. Second, with the help of Torrance, I read 1 Corinthians 15 with proper attention. The purpose of the atonement, I learned, was not negative. It certainly included a powerful negative component, a reaction, an undoing, a doing away with, a judgment against, but Torrance helped me to listen to the apostle, to learn that the work of Christ is first and foremost a creative act, a joyful act, a life-giving act. As Calvin puts it, "our redemption would be imperfect if he did not lead us ever onward to the final goal of salvation."[54]

53. Of course, a much longer argument must be made to defend this point, but we have at least sketched an outline to put into dialogue with recent works on the subject.

54. Calvin, *Institutes* II.xvi.1 (p. 503). In this way, Calvin locates the satisfaction of God's wrath and God's judgment within a larger picture of salvation.

Paul tells us that, apart from the resurrection, not only is our faith futile, but we are in fact still in our sins (1 Cor. 15:17). Freedom from sin cannot be a matter of merely removing punishment; something else, something greater, is required. And that has to do with more than death. "For since death came through a man" would lead you to expect something like, "death was undone by the death of a man." But Paul tells us something rather different: "The resurrection of the dead comes also through a man. For as in Adam all die, so in Christ all will be made alive" (15:21–22 NIV). According to the martyr Polycarp, Christians love him "who died on our behalf"—indeed!—but him likewise who "was raised by God for our sakes."[55] God's response to our sin is not something neutral, a mere undoing, a destruction; rather, it is something altogether stronger and more joyful than that. To be free of our sins is to be made alive, to be resurrected, to be raised in glory and power, to be raised as a spiritual body (1 Cor. 15:42–44). Why did God become man? That in him we might be raised to new life. "The third day a new life of Jesus begins; but at the same time on the third day there begins a new *Aeon*, a new shape of the world, after the old world has been completely done away and settled in the death of Jesus Christ."[56] What is the content of the "oneness" in at-one-ment? That we (and all of the new creation) might be one as he is one (John 17), that we might be one in him, in his glory, his power, his love, his Spirit. This—the fulfillment of the creation narrative in the power of the indwelling Spirit—is our true justification, Paul tells us (Rom. 4:25).

"He Ascended to Heaven"

What does it mean to be human, and what is our destiny? The answer, according to the Christian faith, is not available to us primarily through the social sciences and humanities, as important as

---

55. *To the Philippians* 9.2, in M. Holmes, *Apostolic Fathers in English*, 139.
56. Barth, *Dogmatics in Outline*, 122.

they may be and as much as they may help us understand ourselves. Simply put, nature is not a bond, not a limit—it is itself a gift of grace, limited only by the ways in which grace will grace it. What is the telos, the end and goal of human nature? That it might be graced with a completion not available to it by its own means and resources, that it might be so graced by the triune God as to ascend with Christ—to live a graced creaturely existence, to be raised imperishable and spiritual (1 Cor. 15:42–44).[57] Jesus ascends to the Father's right hand because this completes the movement and pattern of glory and grace that are spoken of in Jesus's high-priestly prayer and echoed throughout Scripture. As Barth puts it, "The end of His work is that we are with Him above. We with Him beside God."[58] The goal of nature is not nature but graced nature, for the root and end of nature is the same, the grace and election of God in Christ. The goal is graced or purified nature, not only on earth but in "the heavenly things as well."[59]

"From There He Will Come to Judge the Living and the Dead"

There is a judgment to come; the whole New Testament is angled so as to build momentum in this direction. God will come among us, bringing final judgment. Jesus's teachings speak of his coming again, his judgment, and the separation of people to his right hand of blessing and to his left hand of judgment (Matt. 25:31–33). Paul's writing, along similar lines, is replete with visions of a final judgment (Rom. 2:5–16; 2 Cor. 5:10). God, in his patience, holds back his judgment and gives people and the nations time to know and respond to him. But who is this one who comes to judge? Who is the one who is worthy? "Worthy is the Lamb, who was slain, / to receive power and wealth and wisdom and strength / and honor and glory

---

57. Calvin, *Institutes* II.xvi.16 (p. 525).
58. Barth, *Dogmatics in Outline*, 125. Cf. Farrow, *Ascension Theology*, 122.
59. Farrow, *Ascension Theology*, 123. On atonement and the ascension, see Moffitt, *Atonement and the Logic of Resurrection*.

and praise!" (Rev. 5:12 NIV). The atonement is an act of making-at-one, but it is such as an act of judgment. Those established in the ways and justice of God, those justified in him, experience the new and spiritual life of the resurrection. Those who reject the ways and justice of God, who reject the Messiah, experience the judgment from which he came to save them. The testimony to this judgment is twofold, both in the tangible form of the burden borne by Christ and in the prophetic-apostolic telling of that which is to come. The joy, honor, and glory with which God is who he is, which he seeks to share with us, is the intensity with which he rejects those who reject him.

"I Believe in the Holy Spirit"

To move to the third article of the creed is not to cease to reflect on Jesus and his work, for his work is intended to prepare for the Holy Spirit and to share him with us. As Jesus prepares his disciples for his death and resurrection, he tells them, "But very truly I tell you, it is for your good that I am going away. Unless I go away, the Advocate will not come to you; but if I go, I will send him to you" (John 16:7 NIV). The atonement is not merely a matter of removing our sin, removing the barriers between ourselves and the Father; the goal was and is far greater than that: that we might be holy as he is holy (Lev. 19:2). This can sound, of course, like we try to be as similar to God as we are able, that we imitate his character. But Jesus is clear: there is no being like God apart from being in and with God. It is only by the power of God, in relationship to God, participating in God, that we become like him. So that we can be holy as he is holy, God gives us his Holy Spirit, which grants us a life, accordingly, "in full and perfect peace."[60] This, of course, demands that we reframe our understanding of the cross: it is God's preparatory work, his cleansing of the temple that it might be a good and fitting receptacle for

---

60. Augustine, *Augustine Catechism*, 140.

the promised Spirit, that we might be holy as he is holy.[61] But more of this in chapter 4.

"I Believe in the Holy Catholic Church and the Communion of Saints"

Scripture does not allow us to hold our belief in the holy catholic church at any distance from Christ's atoning work. God became man to reconcile all things in heaven and on earth to himself (Col. 1:20). And what of those "things" in their reconciled status? To them is given not merely benefit or privilege but ministry and calling. "All this is from God, who reconciled us to himself through Christ and gave us the ministry of reconciliation: that God was reconciling the world to himself in Christ, not counting people's sins against them. And he has committed to us the message of reconciliation" (2 Cor. 5:18–19 NIV). The church, Paul tells us, has been given the ministry of reconciliation that we might be the word and deed, the ambassadors, the images or icons, of Christ.

And to be clear, these are damning words indeed. Just today I heard some catastrophically grievous news of one of God's churches participating in sin and harm worthy, if anything is, of God's punishment of Sodom and Gomorrah. Here, too, we stand on the ground of belief, of faith. We believe in the church, not as the basis of our belief (as that in which we trust and to which we are faithful in a manner parallel to our faith in God) but as a calling of our God, who has wooed a people to himself and given them a vocation, the ministry of reconciliation—to take up the burdens and hurts and sins of others—the ministry of being an image of the image of God, that we might be a part of the making-one of all things. Our belief in the church is a belief in the God of the church, as well as in his purpose and calling for it as the body of the crucified and risen Lord, the body that he has given his Holy Spirit.

---

61. Moffitt, *Rethinking the Atonement*, 254.

"I Believe in the Forgiveness of Sins"

The atoning work of Jesus is a work of his love, a love he specifies as being an internal reality extended outward. "Love your neighbor as [you love] yourself" (Matt. 22:39 NIV). The root of this action is the eternal life of God—the internal reality that God extends outward to his creation in and through his involvement in his creation, in his preserving, accompanying, and redeeming work. The work of the church, its ministry of reconciliation, bears the same fundamental shape. The work of the church is rooted in the internal reality of the joy and shared work of its membership, their interconnected and mutually dependent lives—supporting, caring, worshiping, and (in short) living out the reality of God's life among themselves as God's holy and righteous people.

But as with our previous point about the ministry of reconciliation, so, too, the people of God are who they are through the forgiveness of sins. Scripture's witness about forgiveness is a daunting synthesis of immeasurable gift and fierce demand, which can be summed up in the command to "be kind and compassionate to one another, forgiving each other, just as in Christ God forgave you" (Eph. 4:32 NIV). Kindness and compassion are beautiful and life-giving, of course, but the calling of God is no easy task and is described as dying to self for a reason. First, forgiveness comes as a command bordering on a threat: "If you do not forgive others their sins, your Father will not forgive your sins" (Matt. 6:15 NIV). Forgiveness may be an act of unconditional love, but it is unconditionally demanded of us—a sine qua non of participation in Christ. Second—and this point is even harder than the first—we are to forgive not merely by letting go, not merely by not demanding punishment or restitution; we are to forgive "just as in Christ God forgave you" (Eph. 4:32 NIV). For "the way of the Christian is derived from the forgiveness of sins and leads to the resurrection of the body and eternal life."[62] We will explore this haunting point in much greater depth in chapter 5.

---

62. Barth, *Dogmatics in Outline*, 149.

"I Believe in the Resurrection of the Body and the Life Everlasting"

The creed begins by affirming our belief in "God the Father almighty, creator of heaven and earth," and it ends by reaffirming that original creative impetus. The atonement is not merely a solution to a problem, a repealing or abolishing of a negative state of affairs, for the simple reason that there is no neutral ground that preceded sin to which we could return. Creation is what it is in, by, through, and for its maker. The creed ends by affirming the resurrection of the body and of life everlasting because these comprise the conclusive, delightful, and comprehensive satisfaction of the good pleasure of God: to be the God of a creation and of creatures who are in his image, who through participation in him, by participation "in His nature, in His life and essence,"[63] extend his character into a new and different sphere, the sphere of creatures and their relationships with each other and with him. As Calvin puts it, "Transfusing us with his power," God "quicken[s] us to spiritual life, sanctif[ies] us by his Spirit, [and] adorn[s] his church with divers gifts of grace."[64]

And this life in Christ through his Spirit to the glory of the Father is a life everlasting for the simple reason that Christ came to take the death that was ours so that we could have the life that is his—everlasting life. The life we have in him is not merely a matter of "getting in" to some new state or of preserving bodily function and integrity as we know it; rather, it is a matter of participating in God, of abiding and partaking in him who is the way, the truth, and the life (John 14:6)—the one to whom it has been granted that he have life in himself, just as the Father has life in himself (5:26). What satisfies God? Surely no mere negative state of affairs will do. No mere punishment. No doing away with the source of trouble and wrong. No blank slate. God is satisfied, God delights, God's joy overflows first and foremost in his sharing of himself as the triune God that he

63. Barth, *Dogmatics in Outline*, 45.
64. Calvin, *Institutes* II.xvi.16 (p. 525).

is—Father, Son, and Holy Spirit. And the second is like it: God is satisfied, God delights, God's joy overflows in his sharing of himself with his creatures, that by being in and with him we might be like him, that we might participate in that which he properly is, that we might have everlasting life, that we might be holy and righteous as he is holy and righteous, that we might love as he loves.

And this—this will be very, very good.

DOXOLOGICAL INTERLUDE

George Herbert's "The Sacrifice"

OH all ye, who passe by, whose eyes and minde
To worldly things are sharp, but to me blinde;
To me, who took eyes that I might you finde:
 Was ever grief like mine?

Without me each one, who doth now me brave,
Had to this day been an Egyptian slave.
They use that power against me, which I gave:
 Was ever grief like mine?

The Priest and rulers all false witnesse seek
'Gainst him, who seeks not life, but is the meek
And readie Paschal Lambe of this great week:
 Was ever grief like mine?

Some said, that I the Temple to the floore
In three dayes raz'd, and raised as before.
Why, he that built the world can do much more:
 Was ever grief like mine?

My silence rather doth augment their crie;
My dove doth back into my bosome flie,
Because the raging waters still are high:
 Was ever grief like mine?

Why, Caesar is their onely King, not I:
He clave the stonie rock, when they were drie;
But surely not their hearts, as I well trie:
    Was ever grief like mine?

Then on my head a crown of thorns I wear:
For these are all the grapes *Sion* doth bear,
Though I my vine planted and watred there:
    Was ever grief like mine?

So sits the earths great curse in *Adams* fall
Upon my head: so I remove it all
From th' earth unto my brows, and bear the thrall:
    Was ever grief like mine?

Then with the reed they gave to me before,
They strike my head, the rock from thence all store
Of heav'nly blessings issue evermore:
    Was ever grief like mine?

O all ye who passe by, behold and see;
Man stole the fruit, but I must climbe the tree;
The tree of life to all, but onely me:
    Was ever grief like mine?

They give me vineger mingled with gall,
But more with malice: yet, when they did call,
With Manna, Angels food, I fed them all:
    Was ever grief like mine?

But now I die; now all is finished.
My wo, mans weal: and now I bow my head.
Onely let others say, when I am dead,
    Never was grief like mine.[1]

---

1. Stanzas 1, 3, 15, 17, 24, 31, 41–43, 51, 60, 63. See https://ccel.org/h/herbert/temple/Sacrifice.html.

CHAPTER TWO

Scripture

OUR GOAL IN THIS CHAPTER is to learn to think with Scripture about the meaning and significance of the death and resurrection of Jesus—for Scripture has a "mind," a pattern of thought that shapes and informs the text.[1] And to paraphrase Paul, it is by offering our minds to God as a living sacrifice, conforming them to the reality of God's mercy in Jesus, that we offer true and proper worship. We worship; we properly offer back to God in joy and thanksgiving a mind conformed to the mind of God revealed in the mind of Scripture. Guided by the ruled reading of the church as embedded in the Apostles' Creed, we dive into the interpretation of Scripture.

At the very least, this pattern of thinking with Scripture entails (1) surveying the relevant biblical material on the doctrine of the atonement—considering some of the most important passages in Scripture pertaining to Christ's passion so that they can guide and norm our thought—and (2) familiarizing ourselves with the language the Old and New Testaments employ to speak of Christ's work. This approach would take us into Genesis 3 and its prophecy that a son of Eve would crush the head of the serpent, Leviticus 16 and the Day of Atonement, Psalm 22's cry of dereliction, Isaiah 53's suffering

---

1. "For Athanasius discernment of the mind of scripture meant discovering its underlying coherence, its unitive testimony to the one true Son of God." Young, "The 'Mind' of Scripture," 127.

servant, the Gospel narratives of the passion of Christ and Christ's
prophecies preceding and preparing for them, and Romans 3 and
2 Corinthians 5, among others. We would also need to do lexical
work on the meaning of *kipper*, *katallagē*, *lytron*, and so on. And
in doing this we would be following well-trodden paths.[2] Biblical
commentaries and sermons by Chrysostom, Augustine, Thomas
Aquinas, Luther, and Calvin, not to mention a world of scholarship
in the twentieth and twenty-first centuries, should guide and refine
our thinking, with the help of focused works by biblical scholars and
systematic theologians.

But while our goal certainly affirms and even presupposes these two
approaches, it does not stop there. In fact, this is only the beginning,
for our goal is not merely to think *about* Scripture and what it says but
to think *with* it—to put it in Burroughs's terms, to learn to see with
and through Scripture. Our goal is to follow its logic, to adapt to its
patterns of thought, and to conform to the ways that God, through
his inspired word, wants to guide our thinking and worship concerning the saving work of Jesus in his death and resurrection—and the
way that he both discloses and fulfills the "single, sprawling, complex
but essentially coherent narrative" of the Bible.[3] To do that, we will
certainly consider some of the main passages and words pertaining to
atonement, but we begin by attending to five of the New Testament's
central commitments that guide its thinking about the work of Christ.

Five Central Commitments

First, we begin with the road to Emmaus (Luke 24:25–32), for Scripture thinks of Christ's atonement not abstractly, merely in terms of the

---

2. See, for instance, the relevant sections of Hill and James, *Glory of the Atonement*; Morris,
Apostolic Preaching of the Cross; Brown, *Death of the Messiah*.
3. N. T. Wright, *Paul and the Faithfulness of God*, 2:116; Torrance, *Atonement*, 2. Cf.
Bonino, *Reading the Song of Songs with St. Thomas Aquinas*, 7. For an example of the kind of
hermeneutic I employ here, see Boersma, *Scripture as Real Presence*; Jamieson and Wittman,
Biblical Reasoning. Throughout this book, I assume a canonical approach to Scripture; see, for
example, Moberly, *Old Testament Theology*, 155–62; Vanhoozer, *Drama of Doctrine*, 115–242.

efficacy of the death of the God-man, but in terms of his fulfillment of the Old Testament, in which the "gospel is 'pre-proclaimed' in advance (Gal. 3:8; cf. Rom. 1:2), and that proclamation prior to Christ is a necessary element within all proclamation after Christ."[4] Walking to Emmaus, the risen Jesus says to two disciples, "'O foolish ones, and slow of heart to believe all that the prophets have spoken! Was it not necessary that the Christ should suffer these things and enter into his glory?' And beginning with Moses and all the Prophets, he interpreted to them in all the Scriptures the things concerning himself" (Luke 24:25–27). It was necessary that Christ suffer and enter into his glory—a necessity rooted in Moses and all the prophets (cf. John 5:39–47). The Old Testament, according to Jesus, concerns himself; the Scriptures "bear witness" about him (John 5:39); what happened to him was "in accordance with the Scriptures" (1 Cor. 15:3–4); and Christ himself takes away the veil so that we can understand the old covenant properly (2 Cor. 3:14–16). *Our first point, then, is that to understand the mind of Scripture concerning the death and resurrection of Jesus, we must understand the Old Testament's holistic witness to him*—"all the Scriptures" and "all that the prophets have spoken."[5]

We could take this to mean that we should observe those places in the New Testament that explain the prophecies of Christ's passion in the Old Testament. But Scripture has something much bigger in mind. Jesus, in John 17:20–24, prays to the Father:

> I do not ask for these only, but also for those who will believe in me through their word, that they may all be one, just as you, Father, are in me, and I in you, that they also may be in us, so that the world may believe that you have sent me. The glory that you have given me I have given to them, that they may be one even as we are one, I in them and you in me, that they may become perfectly one, so that the

---

4. Watson, "Paul and Scripture," 358. The road to Emmaus is precisely where John Behr thinks we should begin. Behr, *Mystery of Christ*, 21–26.

5. This includes but is not limited to an allegorical interpretation of the Old Testament, such as we see in Gal. 4:24.

world may know that you sent me and loved them even as you loved me. Father, I desire that they also, whom you have given me, may be with me where I am, to see my glory that you have given me because you loved me before the foundation of the world.

The logic of the prayer stretches back before the foundation of the world, to the life of the triune God as Father, Son, and Holy Spirit, and it extends that dynamic of oneness (recall the Shema from Deut. 6:4—"Hear, O Israel: The Lord our God, the Lord is one") and glory (think of Exod. 40) to those for whom the Son was sent. The logic of the atonement (present here in the form of "sending," which, for John, is bound up with the cross) is not merely one of solving the problem of sin but also one of solving the problem of creation: we creatures becoming as God is that we might image, portray, the maker of heaven and earth, being one as he is one and glorious as he is glorious. This same pattern of thought is at play in the refrain "Be holy as I am holy" (e.g., Lev. 19:2) and in Ephesians 1, where the Lord Jesus Christ, in whom we were chosen "before the foundation of the world" (v. 4), is the means by which God shares with us what he is: the Son is the means by which we receive adoption as sons and daughters. The atonement, according to Scripture, is bigger than the passages that speak directly about it. Rather, it is as big as the doctrine of God, for the goal of the atonement is that we be as the God of Abraham, Isaac, and Jacob is. *Our second point, then, is that Scripture demands that our doctrine of the atonement have the whole doctrine of God in play—the God who revealed himself in his history with his chosen people, Israel.*

To do justice to the mind of Scripture, we must complement our emphasis on the God of Israel with Israel's identity and worship, for Jesus, according to the New Testament and particularly the Letter to the Hebrews, is the reality underlying the central features of Jewish identity. Jesus is the great high priest (Heb. 3–9);[6] he is the

---

6. I do not cover Christ's priestly work in depth in this book. See Torrance, *Atonement*, 61–96; Barth, *CD* IV/1, 275–83; Moffitt, *Rethinking the Atonement*; Fletcher-Louis, "High Priest in Ben Sira 50."

better sacrifice, and his blood the better blood (12:24); he is the new covenant (Luke 22:20). But Jesus is not merely new and better; the proper distinction is between the copy or shadow and the heavenly reality (Heb. 8:5; 9:23–28). And the copy or shadow was built according to the pattern, the heavenly reality, shown to Moses on the mountain (8:5). In other words, the law, Proverbs, the temple, and the sacrificial system—all the distinctive features of Israel's life and worship—were built on the pattern of Jesus Christ, who is their ultimate and heavenly reality. For this reason, Jesus is "the cornerstone for understanding the Scriptures and for explaining and expositing them. The cross grounds theological speech."[7] The new that fulfills the old is in fact the original pattern upon which the old was built. Given this reality, the death and resurrection of Jesus take on new meaning, for his passion is an event in the life of the incarnate heavenly pattern, fulfilling the meaning of the earthly shadow, "mobiliz[ing] the entire body of Scripture."[8] *Our third point concerning the mind of Scripture, then, is that the death and resurrection of Jesus are the fulfillment of Israel's identity, history, and worship precisely because he is the fundamental reality that these imitate and by which they are brought to completion.*

But this third point could unduly limit us to an emphasis on Israel and on Israel's role among the nations—an anthropocentric emphasis. According to the mind of Scripture, the work of Christ is about far more than this. Ephesians 1:9–10 tells us of "the mystery of [God's] will, according to his purpose, which he set forth in Christ as a plan for the fullness of time, to unite all things in him, things in heaven and things on earth." Scripture is not just about Israel (recall Gen. 12:3—"In you *all* the families of the earth shall be blessed"—and the concern for the nations resounding through the prophets), though it is about things in, through, and for God's chosen people. Rather, Scripture is about the flourishing of creation as such: heaven and

7. Venard, *Poetic Christ*, 342.
8. Venard, *Poetic Christ*, 354.

earth, plant and beast, Jew and gentile. And God's plan is to accomplish this flourishing in his Son, the "image of the invisible God," by whom "all things were created, in heaven and on earth, visible and invisible . . . —all things were created through him and for him. And he is before all things, and in him all things hold together" (Col. 1:15–17; cf. 1 Cor. 8:6). *Our fourth point about the mind of Scripture, then, is that it has a cosmic emphasis, looking to the completion of creation, of all things in heaven and on earth, through the work of the Messiah, the promised one of Israel.*

This brings us to our final reflection: this Jesus, "for whom and by whom all things exist," is the one who "by the grace of God" tasted suffering and death for everyone (Heb. 2:9–10). The one by whom and for whom all things were created, the one in whom all creation holds together, the one who in himself sums up and fulfills the identity of Israel, suffered and died to bring his creation to perfection. The New Testament looks to Jesus as the one Israelite by whom and in whom creation is brought to completion precisely by means of his death and resurrection. A twofold dynamic shapes all of Scripture's thinking concerning the Messiah: (1) in this one's crucifixion, the whole negative trajectory of God's relationship to fallen creation—suffering, judgment, and death—is completed, and (2) in this one's resurrection occurs an even greater completion of God's whole creative project. *Our fifth point in summing up the mind of Scripture, then, is that Jesus fulfills the Old Testament as (1) the one in whom all things suffer the fate of reality under sin before God (Gen. 2:17) and (2) the one in whom creation is remade before God in the fullness of his blessing (2 Cor. 5:17; Col. 1:15).*

To recapitulate, our goal is not to go directly to (what seem to be) the main passages concerning the death and resurrection of Jesus, nor to the main words, images, and concepts used to explain his passion. Rather, we want to learn to think with Scripture about the atoning work of Christ, guided by Scripture's most fundamental commitments. In the long run, only such an approach, a dialectic in which we harmonize the mind of Scripture with those passages that speak of or interpret Christ's passion, will give us a full understanding. While we could easily devote a whole book to the subject, for the sake of the present project we will gather the above insights into the following summary:

> To understand the mind of Scripture concerning the death and resurrection of Jesus, (1) we must understand the Old Testament's holistic witness to him (2) within the larger framework of the being and purposes of the God who revealed himself in his history with his chosen people, Israel—and therefore (3) the way that, in his death and resurrection, Jesus is the fulfillment of Israel's identity, history, and worship precisely because he is the fundamental reality that these imitate and by which they are brought to completion. Scripture takes this particular approach to (4) what is ultimately a cosmic emphasis, looking to the completion of all things in heaven and on earth, (5) through the work of the Messiah as (a) the one in whom all things suffer the fate of reality under sin before God and (b) the one in whom creation is remade before God in the fullness of his blessing.

This access into the mind of Scripture comes primarily from the New Testament (though it begins with the Pentateuch's interpretation of itself and the Prophets' interpretation of the Pentateuch), but the content comes primarily from the Old Testament. For it is in his history with Israel that God establishes both his identity and the substance of that which reaches fulfillment in Christ. An account of the death and resurrection of the God-man will not suffice, for the generic will always fall short of the particular when it comes to the self-revelation of God and his will as the Lord of all creation, as the one who chose to bless and complete his fallen creation through his chosen people, Israel, and its Messiah.[9]

9. This, I take it, is one of the great weaknesses of Anselm's *Why God Became Man*: the way it fails to engage the particular content of Scripture and more particularly of Israel. At best, it significantly veils the realities. Thomas Aquinas, on the other hand, follows a much better logic in this regard. Cf. Levering, *Christ's Fulfillment of Torah and Temple*.

The remainder of the chapter will outline, in varying amounts of detail, some of the particular aspects of Israel's identity and worship that Jesus fulfills, in a way that both honors what Christ may have said to the disciples on the road to Emmaus and shapes some of the fundamental doctrinal commitments within a biblical understanding of the atonement.[10] In doing so, we will only touch on some of the most famous passages in the Bible regarding the atonement, for our goal is to adopt a whole pattern of thinking and seeing, that we might be transformed by the renewing of our minds—a beautiful form of worship.

Covenant

God electing to be the God of a nation, the God of Abraham, Isaac, Jacob, and the people that came from them, is the defining feature of Israel's existence and, therefore, of the doctrine of the atonement.[11] God, the maker of heaven and earth, chooses—elects—to be their God and to accomplish his purposes through them. And God graces and adorns this choice with a covenant, a binding promise accompanied by signs and a memorial.[12] This covenant, repeated and amplified over the course of Israel's history with God, is the external basis for all that occurs within their relationship—the outer perimeter, the boundary, the thing that gives shape and purpose to all that occurs within it.[13] The judges, priests, sacrifices and tabernacle, laws, kings, festivals—everything distinctive about the people of Israel occurs within the framework established by the covenant God makes and upholds with his people to be their God and to dwell with them in a promised land (Gen. 12; Exod. 6) in the midst of the nations.

10. For works particularly sensitive to the role of the Old Testament in the doctrine of the atonement, see Torrance, *Atonement*; C. J. H. Wright, "Atonement in the Old Testament"; Leithart, *Delivered from the Elements of the World*.
11. Barth, *CD* IV/1, 3–78; Gorman, *Death of the Messiah*.
12. McKnight, "Covenant."
13. On the "internal" and "external" distinction, see Barth, *CD* III/1, 94–329.

The prophets interpret the meaning of God's covenant with Israel in terms of a marriage.[14] As a husband and his wife are united, so is God with Israel. God rescues Israel out of bondage in Egypt—a time in which she grows and matures as a people (Ezek. 16:7)—and leads her into the desert, where he marries and makes a covenant with her (16:8). And God loves his wife, cleansing and adorning her, until her renown goes out among the nations (16:10–14). And this renown is likewise God's renown, for his covenant with Israel is his chosen means of establishing his name among the peoples—whom he plans to bless through Israel.

But with this intimacy comes another aspect of God's love: his jealousy.[15] The passages exploring God's covenant with Israel resound with the refrain that he is a jealous God whom we should fear. Just after the Shema, God warns Israel:

> Take care lest you forget the LORD, who brought you out of the land of Egypt, out of the house of slavery. It is the LORD your God you shall fear. Him you shall serve and by his name you shall swear. You shall not go after other gods, the gods of the peoples who are around you—for the LORD your God in your midst is a jealous God—lest the anger of the LORD your God be kindled against you, and he destroy you from off the face of the earth. (Deut. 6:12–15)

And this is precisely the theme that the prophets (Ezekiel in particular) explore in light of the sin and idolatry of Israel: the wrath of the jealous God, the spurned lover of Israel (cf. Ezek. 6–7; 23; Jer. 3; 16; Hosea).[16]

> Therefore, O prostitute, hear the word of the LORD: Thus says the Lord GOD, Because your lust was poured out and your nakedness uncovered in your whorings with your lovers, and with all your

14. Cf. Luther, *Freedom of a Christian*, 408–11.
15. Webster, *Holiness*, 50–51.
16. Yang and Davis, "Atonement and the Wrath of God"; Marshall, *Aspects of the Atonement*, 1–67.

abominable idols, . . . behold, I will gather all your lovers with whom
you took pleasure . . . and will uncover your nakedness to them, that
they may see all your nakedness. And I will judge you as women who
commit adultery and shed blood are judged, and bring upon you the
blood of wrath and jealousy. . . . So will I satisfy my wrath on you, and
my jealousy shall depart from you. (Ezek. 16:35–38, 42)

To be sure, this is not the end of the story as the prophets envision it,
but it must carry its proper weight. We must not pass over it. After
God has withdrawn his gifts and protection, exposed her to her lovers, and poured out his wrath upon her, he returns to her, allures and
speaks tenderly to her, establishing a new covenant, betrothing her
forever in righteousness and justice, in steadfastness, and in mercy
(Hosea 2:14–23).

Scholars will sometimes seek to connect the doctrine of penal
substitution with the sacrificial system.[17] But as we will see, this
connection rests on a misunderstanding of categories with which
sacrifices work. The true basis for penal substitution, for the emphasis on the wrath of God and his punishment of sin, is not the
sacrificial system but the covenants of God—the external basis of
God's relationship with his people. For who is Jesus but the one who
in and of himself takes up the history of Israel before her husband?
Who is Jesus but the one who is stripped naked before the nations,
bearing the shame? Who is the one upon whom God satisfies his
wrath (Ezek. 16:42)? None other than Jesus, who, in order to win
for himself a bride, takes the place of his bride—the one who in
her folly spurned him as a lover, running after other gods, whoring
herself out to them.

The consistent witness of the Old Testament is that for Israel to
break its covenant with God is for it to incur not merely God's ab-

---

17. Hodge, for instance, writes that "if the ordinary authoritative rules of interpretation
are to be adhered to, it cannot be denied that the Scriptures teach that Christ saves us as a
priest by making a full expiation for our sins, bearing the penalty of them in his own person
in our behalf" (Hodge, *Systematic Theology*, 2:498). For a more nuanced version of this point,
see Bavinck, *Reformed Dogmatics*, 3:396.

sence, not merely a host of natural consequences stemming from a broken relationship with nature (though these are certainly included), but ultimately God's jealous wrath and judgment. For the covenantal bond between the two to be honored in the midst of Israel's dishonor, faithlessness, and adultery is for God to respond in jealousy, wrath, and judgment (Deut. 28:15–68; Josh. 24:14–28; Ezek. 23:22–27; Hosea 2:1–13). Wrath and judgment are the power and intimacy of the covenant directed toward one who breaks that covenant. And Jesus, who for us was made to be sin, takes upon himself the fate of Israel. But that, as we have seen, is not the final word, for the Old Testament vacillates in two seemingly contradictory directions, particularly when it comes to the prophets: "I will destroy," says the Lord (Hosea 4:5)—and "I will heal" (14:4). Which will it be? And how can this be? The answer, according to the New Testament, is that only both in their completeness will satisfy God: both satisfy his wrath and jealousy but, greater still, satisfy his love.[18] Only full judgment and death will do, and—God be praised!—only resurrection and restoration will do for the establishment of a new and greater covenant.

Law

The law is the internal basis of the covenant; obedience to God (and therefore God's law) was the means by which Israel kept covenant faithfulness.[19] God spoke, and creation came into being—but with humankind, God speaks, and we are to obey. Just before giving Moses the Ten Commandments, God tells the Israelites, "You yourselves have seen what I did to the Egyptians, and how I bore you on eagles' wings and brought you to myself. Now therefore, if you will indeed obey my voice and keep my covenant, you shall be my treasured possession among all peoples, for all the earth is

18. Torrance, *Atonement*, 8–10.
19. N. T. Wright, *The New Testament and the People of God*, 260–61.

mine; and you shall be to me a kingdom of priests and a holy nation" (Exod. 19:4–6). Israel is led in the exodus, receives the law, and then receives the law again after the golden calf incident, and each time the law changes and develops while the connection between obedience and covenant remains the same. To keep covenant is to keep obedience.

The blessings and the curses of the covenant that culminate in Deuteronomy 28 (cf. Lev. 26 and 2 Chron. 7) cement this line of thought. On the one hand is blessing: standing high over the nations of the earth, food in abundance, rain in due season, and so on. Every threat will be removed, and every good thing requisite for life will be in abundance—as long as Israel does not turn aside from what God commands. And on the other hand stand curses—an overwhelming list of afflictions and sufferings in every area of life, including land, marriage, family, and the nations, summed up in a reversal of Genesis 3: "If in spite of this you will not listen to me, but walk contrary to me, then I will walk contrary to you in fury, and I myself will discipline you sevenfold for your sins" (Lev. 26:27–28). Well-being, for the nation of Israel, revolves around obeying the word of the Lord and his commandments—and thereby keeping covenant faithfulness.

But Israel knows that while faithfulness is possible, it will not happen. Moses tells them as much in Deuteronomy 28–30.[20] But he simultaneously anticipates something far greater: a time when a new covenant will be made that will be accompanied once more by the means of keeping covenant faithfulness (Deut. 30). But this time, the law will be written on their hearts (Jer. 31:31–40), such that there will be no more need to remember, to teach—for the people will act out of the law on their hearts, and covenant will be kept with all its attending blessings. All along, Israel was to love God with all its heart (Deut. 6:5), but now that heart will be remade. The content of this obedience we will see in other sections (on sacrifice, Sabbath,

---

20. N. T. Wright, *Climax of the Covenant*, 145–46.

etc.); at present, we merely dwell on the fact of the law and the call to obedience, with the blessings and curses of walking with or against the maker of heaven and earth in the balance.

But Jesus is the fulfillment of this reality, for he is the end, the telos, of the law (Rom. 10:4). He is the righteousness of God among us, the heart of God, who came not to abolish but to fulfill the law (Matt. 5:17), for he came to fulfill himself and his place within creation.[21] And much like the priesthood is fulfilled by one outside the line of priests (i.e., in the order of Melchizedek), so now the root and telos of the law, the righteousness of God, "has been manifested apart from the law, although the Law and the Prophets bear witness to it" (Rom. 3:21). The work of Christ was to manifest and reveal God's righteousness that God might be "just and the justifier" (3:26), or righteous and the righteous-maker (δίκαιον καὶ δικαιοῦντα), as the one who shares his own being as the very image of God (Col. 1:15) and his righteousness with those he makes in his image. Jesus's death and resurrection are the fulfillment of the law.

Sabbath

The Sabbath—built into the structure of creation as the seventh day, on which God rested from his work (Gen. 2:1–3), and incorporated into the rhythm of the people of Israel in the exodus (Exod. 16:23–29) before being instituted as law in the Ten Commandments (20:8–11)—is one of the most significant markers of Israel's life with God.[22] The prophets associate keeping Sabbath with holding fast to the covenant (Isa. 56:4–6), while the failure to keep Sabbath resounds throughout their chastisement of Israel. For this reason, it is disagreement over how to keep the Sabbath properly that is often the point of conflict between Jesus and the Pharisees. Israel is to "remember the Sabbath day, to keep it holy" (Exod. 20:8).

21. This, in many ways, is the animating insight of Athanasius (*On the Incarnation* 6 [p. 63]).
22. Barker, "Sabbath, Sabbatical Year, Jubilee."

The centrality of this commitment is clear from the way that Jeremiah follows Leviticus 26, weaving together the fulfillment of the curses with a prominent role for the Sabbath: the destruction of Jerusalem is a punishment that allows the land to keep the Sabbaths (2 Chron. 36:21; Jer. 17:19–27). In the exodus, God instituted the Sabbath while bringing the people into the promised land. But in their breaking of covenant by not keeping the Sabbath, God reverses these events: rather than walking with them, God walks contrary to them (Lev. 26:28a); instead of the seventh day being a blessing, God visits a sevenfold curse on them (v. 28b); instead of eating manna gathered the day before, they will eat the flesh of their sons and daughters (v. 29); instead of the Sabbath revolving around the worship of God, their sanctuaries will lie desolate, and the altars will be cut down (vv. 30–31). But the land, in God's curse, will enjoy its Sabbath; it will have the rest that Israel was to give it (vv. 34–35).

And what does the atonement have to do with the Sabbath? Genesis makes rest one of the fundamental features of Sabbath. In Psalm 95:11, quoted by Hebrews 3:11 and 4:3, God swears that the people will not "enter my rest." But the possibility of entering that rest still stands (Heb. 4), a rest that could refer to a merely human state or activity but is more properly a reality to be found in Christ. Jesus was dead on the Sabbath; in him, in his experience of Holy Saturday, he experiences the rest that was the judgment of the land. In him, human flesh, the "dust of the ground" (Gen. 2:7 NIV), has its rest, its cessation from all activity, which is a judgment by the forced fulfillment of blessing. In him, we enter the promised rest ("Come to me, . . . and I will give you rest," Matt. 11:28) as new creatures who have died in Christ and put off the works of the flesh. Restless we are until we rest in him, says Augustine.[23] But in Christ we truly are re-created: in his suffering the curse upon Israel and the land for failing to keep Sabbath, and in his being raised to the completion of the Sabbath rest for God's people (Heb. 4:9–10).

23. Augustine, *Confessions*, 3.

Creation and Land

Jesus's fulfillment of the Sabbath invites us to consider an even deeper theme, one that underlies the work we have done thus far. Jesus is not merely the rest into which we enter; he fulfills creation itself and the attending role of the promised land. Ephesians tells of God's plan to "unite all things in [Jesus], things in heaven and things on earth" (1:10); Colossians proclaims that Jesus is the "firstborn of all creation" (1:15); Galatians says that "neither circumcision counts for anything, nor uncircumcision, but a new creation" (6:15); and according to 2 Corinthians 5:17, "If anyone is in Christ, he is a new creation." Linking the logic of these claims, Christ is the firstborn of a new creation and the one through whom God unites all things on earth, making them a new creation. Jesus's resurrection appearance in a garden (Mary thinks he is the gardener in John 20:15), which is the perfect image for the new creation in him, is the appearance of the second Adam, in whom all creation is made new, awaiting his Eve, his bride—the church.

This line of thought is not foreign to the Old Testament. The curse on Adam falls upon the earth (Gen. 3:17). God's judgment on the sin of humankind takes the form of decreation, reversing the events of the six days of creation in the story of the flood (Gen. 6–9)—a theme we see repeated in the Prophets (Isa. 24; Jer. 4:19–31). Humankind is not an accidental feature of creation but its completion, according to Genesis—and the fates of humankind and creation are bound together. The fall has implications for creation, which lies groaning, subject to futility "because of him who subjected it, in hope that the creation itself will be set free from its bondage to corruption and obtain the freedom of the glory of the children of God" (Rom. 8:20–21). Thorns infest the earth:

> Cursed is the ground because of you;
>   in pain you shall eat of it all the days of your life;
> thorns and thistles it shall bring forth for you;
>   and you shall eat the plants of the field. (Gen. 3:17–18)

What does the atonement have to do with creation, with the land? The rightful king of creation enters his realm only to find himself crowned with the very thorns (Matt. 27:29) that choke his creation, his vineyard. The blood he sweats is the great consummation of the sweat with which man was to till the earth, and those thorns are the final harvest of the cursed ground. As Herbert writes:

> Then on my head a crown of thorns I wear:
> For these are all the grapes *Sion* doth bear,
> Though I my vine planted and watred there:
>   Was ever grief like mine?[24]

Enthroned on the tree of death, crowned with the only laurel wreath our wretched and cursed soil could provide, Jesus suffers the fate of cursed creation, bearing the curse of the land upon his brow. And creation responds: shaking, splitting, and being cast into darkness (Matt. 27:45–51). God's punishment for Adam and Eve has come to completion at last.

> So sits the earths great curse in *Adams* fall
> Upon my head: so I remove it all
> From th' earth unto my brows, and bear the thrall:
>   Was ever grief like mine?[25]

But God does not rest content with the thorn; the fall is not the final word. Christ may bear the crown of thorns, but he bears it to remake it, refashioning creation, turning curse into blessing, death to life, thorn to vine. Ezekiel tells of a time bound up with the coming of the Holy Spirit (36:27–38) when the land will become like the garden of Eden: God's people will dwell in the land, and it will be tilled and abundant. The beginning of the fulfillment has happened in the risen Lord, in whom the very dust of the promised land breathes and sits at the right hand of God.

24. Herbert, "The Sacrifice," stanza 41, lines 161–64 (p. 28).
25. Herbert, "The Sacrifice," stanza 42, lines 165–68 (p. 28).

Sacrifice

Jesus is our high priest (Heb. 2:17) and the lamb who takes away the sin of the world (John 1:29). As illustrated by the offerings of Cain and Abel (Gen. 4), the emphasis on clean and unclean animals in the story of Noah (Gen. 6–9), and the binding of Isaac (Gen. 22), sacrifice is woven into the texture of the Pentateuch, taking center stage in Leviticus 1–10. It is tempting to think of sacrifices and offerings in terms of guilt incurred by sin and its corresponding punishment. But while the sacrificial system does have to do with sin and is not unrelated to guilt, the emphasis is not on punishment[26] so much as it is on the holiness of God and God's chosen people and on the cleansing and purification of the people, their possessions, and the land as a whole.[27] In sum, the God-given purpose of the sacrificial system and the host of offerings it entails is to facilitate or enable the holiness of God's people before a holy God. And it is within this context that we explore the relationship between the atonement and sacrifice.

We will begin with the Day of Atonement, when Aaron enters the Holy Place—something done only once a year (Lev. 16:3). Aaron offers sin and burnt offerings, then presents one goat as a sin offering while presenting a second goat alive before the Lord, which is subsequently sent into the wilderness to Azazel. In the process, Aaron makes atonement for the Holy Place, himself, the people, and the altar, with all the emphasis on cleansing the people, the tabernacle, and its items from uncleanness. This is a day of cleansing. The second goat, the one sent into the wilderness, bears the sin that has been confessed over its head and carries it away from the people, offering yet another form of cleansing (that of separation, alongside that of cleansing by blood). Verse 30 sums up the spirit of the day: "For on

26. The role of punishment, as we have seen, pertains to keeping covenant per se, not the sacrificial system as such. It is for this reason that punishment language within Leviticus is found primarily in the final chapters, in a manner corresponding to Deut. 28.

27. N. T. Wright, *The Day the Revolution Began*; Craig, *Atonement and the Death of Christ*, 13–36.

this day shall atonement be made for you to cleanse you. You shall be clean before the LORD from all your sins."

Behind the sacrificial system and the Day of Atonement stands a vision not simply of filth or contamination but of God as holy:[28]

> I am the LORD your God, who has separated you from the peoples. You shall therefore separate the clean beast from the unclean. . . . You shall not make yourselves detestable by beast or by bird or by anything with which the ground crawls, which I have set apart for you to hold unclean. You shall be holy to me, for I the LORD am holy and have separated you from the peoples, that you should be mine. (Lev. 20:24–26)

The holiness of God involves a whole series of separations; just as the waters are separated to make dry land in creation, so the peoples are separated to make room for the people of God. And this separation or set-apartness goes on to characterize every aspect of Israel's existence, as a sign of their holiness before the Holy One of Israel. The sacrificial system, in short, is a God-given means by which Israel can cleanse itself, can maintain its holiness as a holy people before its holy God.[29] The animals are not punished, and the emphasis is not on death. As we have seen, punishment and death play a vital role in the Old Testament and in the work of Christ—but not within the sacrificial system, which is about the manipulation of blood and the cleansing of the people, with the ultimate goal of being in the presence of the Holy One of Israel.[30]

This emphasis on cleansing resounds throughout the New Testament in its witness to Christ. As John the Baptist says, Jesus is the lamb "who takes away the sin of the world" (John 1:29), removing it from the midst of the people; "the blood of Jesus . . . cleanses us from all sin" (1 John 1:7), and we are "washed . . . in the blood of the

---

28. Webster, *Holiness*; Torrance, *Atonement*, 31–32.
29. Torrance, *Atonement*, 19.
30. Moffitt, *Rethinking the Atonement*.

Lamb" (Rev. 7:14). Do not mistake the emphasis on blood for a penal emphasis; blood, in this line of thought, is what cleanses, what makes a people, a temple, or an altar holy before a holy God. Who, then, is Jesus? He is the sacrificial system as a whole.[31] He is an offering to the Lord. He is the high priest (Heb. 2:17) and sacrifice (12:24). Jesus is both goats from the Day of Atonement: he is the one who bears the sins of his people away from them and the one whose blood cleanses them, the gift of the holy God to cleanse his people from their sin that they might be holy as he is holy.[32] And we, as God's holy people, are called to recognize sin for what it is: an uncleanness that defiles and pollutes us, our land, and God's creation, creating barriers, repulsion, and contamination.

Temple

God delights in bringing his people into his presence; the whole point of the sacrificial system is to cleanse, without consuming, his people. God wants to be known and worshiped; he wants us to image him, to be holy as he is holy. He wants to be the God who walks with his people, and he wants his people to be the ones who dwell with him. In Genesis, God comes to walk with Adam and Eve in the cool of the day (Gen. 3:8). In Exodus 3, God comes to Moses in the form of a burning bush, and then he leads the people of Israel from captivity to the promised land. But the culmination of that journey is not the entry into the land, for that is but another beginning. The land must be cleansed and the inheritance possessed—and the turbulent history of Israel in the promised land with God begins, across the ebbs and flows of its relationships with God and his prophets, judges, and kings. But the high point in all this, the high point in the history of Israel, is the building of the temple: the house for the Lord.

---

31. A fuller account would consider the relationship between the atonement and each of the different kinds of offerings, including wave offerings. See Peres, "Bloodless 'Atonement.'"

32. Torrance, *Atonement*, 68.

Prepared by David, Solomon oversees the building of the house
of the Lord (2 Chron. 3–5) and its consecration (2 Chron. 6–7),
offering one of the most beautiful prayers found in the Bible. Then,

> as soon as Solomon finished his prayer, fire came down from heaven
> and consumed the burnt offering and the sacrifices, and the glory
> of the LORD filled the temple. And the priests could not enter the
> house of the LORD, because the glory of the LORD filled the LORD's
> house. When all the people of Israel saw the fire come down and the
> glory of the LORD on the temple, they bowed down with their faces
> to the ground on the pavement and worshiped and gave thanks to the
> LORD, saying, "For he is good, for his steadfast love endures forever."
> (2 Chron. 7:1–3)

Here we see the glory of the Lord as it had been on Mount Sinai and
as it had filled the tabernacle upon its completion during the exodus
(Exod. 40:34). But now it is in the temple, in the city of David, in
the heart of the promised land, when Israel has rest from its enemies,
and the covenant of God with David (and by extension, his covenants
with Abraham, Isaac, Jacob, and Moses) is fulfilled. The glory of the
Lord is in the midst of his chosen people as they respond in worship
and praise—the high point of the people of Israel.

It is not to last, though. The temple is burned to the ground in
Jeremiah 52, and Ezekiel (40–48) culminates in a vision of a new
temple. But what does the death and resurrection of Jesus have to
do with all this?[33] The Word became flesh and "tabernacled" with us
(John 1:14). Jesus, the incarnate Son of God, is the embodied reality the tabernacle and temple were meant to foreshadow. But he
does so in the complex manner of a dual fulfillment: (1) fulfilling
the role of the original tabernacle and (2) fulfilling the pattern upon
which it was based. Jesus bears the fate of the temple's destruction, the

33. Cf. Beale, *The Temple and the Church's Mission*; Hoskins, *Jesus as the Fulfillment of
the Temple*; Levering, *Christ's Fulfillment of Torah and Temple*. See also Anderson, *That I
May Dwell among Them*.

removing of the glory of God and his protective presence, which is the culmination of the theme of God forsaking his people in judgment on their sin (Deut. 31:17–18). God intends to bring his people into his presence, but God's response to a people who forsake him, reject his covenant, and turn to false gods is to forsake them, to withdraw himself from their presence, in judgment, leaving them vulnerable to the nations and forces of nature against which they are defenseless.

But, of course, this is not the end of the story, for God's judgment is ordered toward the establishment of his holiness and righteousness, and his forsaking is ordered toward his restoration of communion and presence. In the resurrection of Jesus, the temple is rebuilt ("I will raise it again in three days," John 2:19 NIV)—the true temple that was the heavenly pattern for the old building—and in him, those united to him are built up into the living temple (2 Cor. 6:16; Eph. 2:19–22).[34] What is the atonement? It is God's work of bringing the reality of the temple to fulfillment in and through Jesus's death and resurrection.

The Exodus and the Nations

Perhaps the most definitive event by which God identifies himself to his people and the nations is the exodus, which is so much more than a mere event in the history of Israel; it is a defining feature of their and their God's identity, anticipated in Genesis, unfolded in the remainder of the Pentateuch, and rehearsed and prophetically employed throughout the Old and New Testaments.[35] Abram and Sarai (Gen. 12:10–20), and later Joseph, preenact the exodus, and the prophets continue to unpack the meaning of the exodus and foretell a future exodus to come (Ezra 1–3; Neh. 1:8–9; Jer. 23:5–8; Hag. 2:1–7). At the heart of the matter are two concerns: (1) God's rescue of his people from captivity to fulfill his covenantal promises

---

34. I offer a much fuller treatment of these topics in Johnson, "Temple Framework of the Atonement"; Johnson, *God's Being in Reconciliation*, 164–96.

35. Graves, "Exodus," 547–48; Moberly, "Exodus, Book of," 211.

and (2) God's establishment of his name among the nations (Exod. 19:4–6; 32:11–14; Num. 14:13–19). One of the surprising ways Scripture employs the exodus is in the form of a threat or judgment (much like the decreation enacted in the flood); the threatened curse in response to covenant faithlessness is that of a reversal of the exodus: "And the LORD will bring you back in ships to Egypt, a journey that I promised that you should never make again; and there you shall offer yourselves for sale to your enemies as male and female slaves, but there will be no buyer" (Deut. 28:68; cf. 2 Chron. 12).

Underlying the exodus, however, is a bigger story: that of Israel and the nations. For the exodus is more than a rescue. Genesis 12 foretells God's blessing of the nations, the families of the earth, through Abraham, which we glimpse in Jacob's blessings of Esau (Gen. 33; "two nations" are in Rebekah's womb [Gen. 25:23]) and Pharaoh (Gen. 47:10–11). It might seem that Genesis 15:14–16 is against this, prophesying the exodus as a judgment of Egypt and the sins of the Amorites (cf. Exod. 15:13–18; Num. 33:4)—evidence, perhaps, of divine favoritism. But Israel lives under the same curse of death (Gen. 2:17) and the same threat: they, too, will be driven out, if they don't drive the nations out (Num. 33:55–56; Deut. 9:6–8). In fact, this happens—and worse than this, Moses teaches Israel that when they sin and provoke God to anger and jealousy, God will in fact use the nations to judge them, just as the exodus had been God's judgment on Egypt. God does this purposefully: "I will make them jealous with those who are no people; / I will provoke them to anger with a foolish nation" (Deut. 32:21).

This is precisely the passage Paul draws from at the heart of his argument in Romans 9–11, explaining the nature of God's election and the role of Israel among the nations in regard to the gospel. Paul's answer: God uses jealousy (Rom. 11:11, 14) to bring about his saving purposes, drawing his chosen people, Israel, to salvation via his blessing of the gentiles (which occurs through their reception of the blessing of the Messiah). The exodus, in other words, has a central role to play within the larger picture of God reversing the consequences of the fall and Babel through his chosen people, in which he "consign[s] all to disobedience, that he may have mercy on all" (11:32).

In a remarkable passage, 1 Corinthians 10 connects the exodus to the work of Christ: he was the spiritual rock that nourished Israel in the desert (v. 4); he was the one who was put to the test by their grumbling (v. 9). Christ was the hidden reality within and behind the exodus. He, according to Jude, both saved Israel out of Egypt and afterward destroyed those who did not believe (Jude 5). Christ, likewise, is the Passover lamb sacrificed for us (1 Cor. 5:7)—the heart of the celebration of the exodus. This theme of the exodus and the nations finds its culmination in Jesus as the one on whose shoulders the government sits (Isa. 9, 11)—a theme made abundantly clear in Mary's Magnificat (Luke 1:46–55) and Simeon's prophecy over the infant Jesus (Luke 2:29–32). But how do the death and resurrection of Jesus relate to Israel and the nations in general and the exodus in particular?

The threat behind the exodus and the role of the nations in Scripture is that God intentionally uses the nations as the means of his judgment for sin (Judg. 2:11–14; 2 Kings 17; 21:12–15). The hope within the exodus and the nations is that God works within the nations to rescue his people from captivity, using his blessing to create a cycle of life-giving jealousy in which blessing begets blessing and nation draws nation into salvation. Jesus's death and resurrection are the fundamental reality in which all these other realities converge. Jesus, taking upon himself the reality of Israel's punishment, is handed over to a foreign empire, Rome, encapsulating in himself the dynamics of exile—God's tool for judging sinful Israel, the fulfillment of the warnings strewn across the pages of the Law and the Prophets. "He was crucified under Pontius Pilate" is no mere historical accident randomly inserted into the Apostles' Creed; it is the culmination of the fate of sinful Israel: being handed over to the nations for judgment, a fitting reversal of the exodus. But likewise, Jesus's resurrection, the triumph over death and the fulfillment of the law, is the great breaking down of the barrier between Jew and gentile, to which Ephesians

2:11–22 and Galatians 3:10–14 bear such beautiful witness. In him is the new and final exodus, through which he will bless (and judge) the nations.

Conclusion

What we have offered to this point is only the briefest sketch of the atonement in Scripture, drawing out some of the ways that Jesus's death and resurrection are the fundamental reality of the major themes of Scripture. We have not attended to the specific prophecies said to be fulfilled in the New Testament (e.g., Matt. 26:56; Luke 22:37; 24:44) or to the connection between the atonement and some of the major figures in the history of Israel, from Adam, Abel, Joseph, and Job to Saul, David, Solomon, the Prophets, and so on.[36] Among these, the book of Job and the way its prologue sets a cosmic stage for what follows—a conflict between God and Satan in which the faithfulness of Job is the testing ground, particularly when seen against the backdrop of Ephesians 3:10 and Colossians 2:15—is especially intriguing.[37] We have left out such themes as circumcision (Gen. 17; Col. 2:11–15), wisdom,[38] kingship (Deut. 17:14–20; 1 Sam. 8:1–18; 1 Chron. 17:10–15; Dan. 7:13–14; Mic. 5:2–5; Mark 15:16–26), and the promised Holy Spirit (1 Sam. 16:14; Ezek. 36–39; Joel 2:29; John 7:39; Acts 2:33). We have hardly touched on the Psalms as a whole, the Servant Songs of Isaiah, or Paul's notion of Christ as the second Adam (Rom. 5).

But given our work in the introduction to this chapter, this should come as no surprise. A single chapter on the atonement in Scripture must not be definitive: it can serve only as a guide to the reader, a part of faith seeking understanding of Holy Scripture—a guide, if you will, to a lifetime of theological "sightseeing." Anything more ambitious will prove to be overly narrow, leaving out themes, concepts,

---

36. Pulse, *Figuring Resurrection*.
37. Barth, *CD* IV/3.1, 368–478; Gregory the Great, *Moralia in Job*.
38. Johnson, *Reconciling Wisdom of God*.

and terms vital to understanding the comprehensive work of Christ. For

> to understand the mind of Scripture concerning the death and resurrection of Jesus, (1) we must understand the Old Testament's holistic witness to him (2) within the larger framework of the being and purposes of the God who revealed himself in his history with his chosen people, Israel—and therefore (3) the way that, in his death and resurrection, Jesus is the fulfillment of Israel's identity, history, and worship precisely because he is the fundamental reality that these imitate and by which they are brought to completion. Scripture takes this particular approach to (4) what is ultimately a cosmic emphasis, looking to the completion of all things in heaven and on earth, (5) through the work of the Messiah as (a) the one in whom all things suffer the fate of reality under sin before God and (b) the one in whom creation is remade before God in the fullness of his blessing.

Theology is meant to nourish the hermeneutical work of the church, "whose only Head is Christ" and who "is born of the Word of God, abides in the same, and does not listen to the voice of a stranger."[39] A chapter such as this, therefore, cannot be a conclusive answer but can only be a reminder and a help in listening to the comprehensive witness of Scripture to the meaning and significance of the death and resurrection of Jesus.

---

39. Cochrane, *Reformed Confessions of the 16th Century*, 49.

DOXOLOGICAL INTERLUDE

Traherne and Barth

The Cross is the abyss of wonders, the centre of desires, the school of virtues, the house of wisdom, the throne of love, the theatre of joys, and the place of sorrows; It is the root of happiness, and the gate of Heaven.[1]

We have to remember the communion of saints, bearing and being borne by each other, asking and being asked, having to take mutual responsibility for and among the sinners gathered together in Christ. As regards theology, also, we cannot be in the Church without taking as much responsibility for the theology of the past as for the theology of our present. Augustine, Thomas Aquinas, Luther, Schleiermacher and all the rest are not dead, but living. They still speak and demand a hearing as living voices, as surely as we know that they and we belong together in the Church. . . . As we make our contribution, they join in with theirs, and we cannot play our part today without allowing them to play theirs. Our responsibility is not only to God, to ourselves, to the men of today, to other living theologians, but to them. There is no past in the Church, so there is no past in theology. "In him they all live." . . . The theology of any period must be strong and free enough to give a calm, attentive and open hearing not only to the voices of the Church Fathers, not only to favourite voices, not only to the voices of the classical past, but to all the voices of the past. God is the Lord of the Church. He is also the Lord of theology.[2]

1. Thomas Traherne, *Centuries of Meditations* 1.58 (p. 39).
2. Barth, *Protestant Theology in the Nineteenth Century*, 3.

CHAPTER THREE

A History of the Doctrine of the Atonement

THE CROSS IS INDEED the abyss of wonders, the center of desires, and the school of virtues, but it takes the communion of saints, "bearing and being borne by each other," together interpreting Scripture, to perceive the cross for what it is, in all its riches. To do theology is to join with our fathers and mothers in the history of the church, for ultimately, "God is the Lord of the Church" and the "Lord of theology." We therefore do theology, we seek to think and speak well of him, by participating in his church, in fellowship with those in the history of the church who, like us, seek to speak well of him. To worship God well, to seek to understand this "root of happiness" and "gate of Heaven," we turn to, among other things, the history of the church's reflection on the doctrine of the atonement.

But prior to F. C. Baur's groundbreaking book on the history of the doctrine of the atonement in 1838, a book such as the one you are reading would not have had a chapter on the history of the doctrine. Irenaeus, Anselm, Calvin—theologians prior to 1838—would cite authorities and interact with contemporaries or heretics, but through-out the history of the church there were no such things as overviews of the atonement that canvassed the main contributors to the doc-trine. This development is a welcome addition to how the doctrine is done, equipping theologians with a host of distinctions, concepts, questions, and patterns of thought that may have been overlooked or forgotten over the years; invigorating the contemporary task; and helping us overcome some of those biases that are so hard to see in ourselves. But this contribution was a complex one, and under-standing its history will help us to correct some of its considerable weaknesses.

Friedrich Schleiermacher is the father of this movement, this em-phasis on the history of doctrine. In the early nineteenth century, as Prussia (Germany) sought to reestablish itself as a global power after its defeat by Napoleon, it launched a campaign to reenvision its university system, particularly at the University of Berlin. Theology, to have a place within this system, had to have a legitimate basis—a scientific one.[1] Schleiermacher provided precisely such an account, locating church doctrine within historical theology, since the "com-munity, regarded as a whole, is a historical entity and . . . its present condition [including its present beliefs or dogmas] can be adequately grasped only when it is viewed as a product of the past."[2] On this basis, "historical theology is the actual corpus of theological study."[3] As we see in Schleiermacher's *The Christian Faith*, the subject matter of Christian dogmatics is not God and God's works but "solely . . . the Christian church,"[4] for only the Christian church can provide the material basis for the scientific approach to the discipline, an ap-proach that would legitimate theology within the newly reenvisioned university system.

1. Purvis, *Theology and the University in Nineteenth-Century Germany*, 2–3. Cf. Howard, *Protestant Theology and the Making of the Modern German University*, 273–302.
2. Schleiermacher, *Brief Outline of Theology*, §26.
3. Schleiermacher, *Brief Outline of Theology*, §28.
4. Schleiermacher, *Christian Faith*, §2, pp. 3–4.

F. C. Baur took up this line of thought. He is "the first historian of religion and dogma to base his comprehensive presentations consistently on the most detailed historical-critical engagement with the sources"[5]—a vision rooted in Schleiermacher's historicization of theology, Niebuhr's detailed historical-critical work, and Hegel's idealist vision of history.[6] Baur's *Die Christliche Lehre von der Versöhnung* is the first comprehensive history of the doctrine of the atonement, a massive and unprecedented work covering the Gnostics, Irenaeus and Origen, John Scotus Eriugena, the scholastic theologians (including Hugh of St. Victor, Scotus, and Wycliffe), the Reformers and Socinians, Hugo Grotius, and others.[7]

But Baur's was an idealistically driven historicism—his interest was in evolutionary development across time.[8] Baur understood his own time to be the scientific-methodical period within "the history of history of dogma," and the challenge was to account for the "external circumstances under which dogma has developed." He sought to trace the "dynamic process" in which this development had occurred, while recognizing that "religious truth can be expressed only approximately in speculative form" and, therefore, that "the history of dogma . . . has to be sensitively discovered from the heartbeat of religious life and the whole organism must be conceived in accord with it."[9] The balance is between legitimate "religious truth," on the one hand, and the speculative form that expresses itself and is

5. Wendte, "Ferdinand Christian Baur," 76.

6. Cf. Wendte, "Ferdinand Christian Baur," 67, 75; Zachhuber, "The Absoluteness of Christianity and the Relativity of All History"; Howard, *Protestant Theology and the Making of the Modern German University*, 278–80.

7. Others were to follow, including Oxenham (1869), Ritschl (1870–74), Sabatier (1903), Rivière (1904), Franks (1918), Grensted (1920), and Aulén (1931).

8. The historical turn "was more than simply the discovery of history." It viewed history as "a web of relationships with contemporaneous, prior, and later developments. It was thus a principle imposing order and sequence." History thus provided "a medium potentially linking [the remains of the past] amongst each other, notably by means of theories of evolutionary development which were as popular in the nineteenth century as they were controversial." Zachhuber, "Historical Turn," 54.

9. Baur, *History of Christian Dogma*, 84.

discovered through the particular "heartbeat of religious life," on the other. Mediating this balance is the scientific category of "theory," the mode in which those "speculative" forms of expression occur. The continuity lies in the development of the heartbeat of religious life, while the distinct theories are diverse, historically determined, and competing speculative expressions of that developing idea or heartbeat.

From Baur to the present day, "theory" language has become the conceptual tool for distinguishing between the different periods and views regarding the atonement. For instance, Baur refers throughout to the "Anselmische Satisfactionstheorie" and the "Lutherischen Theorie," and Gustaf Aulén's famous book *Christus Victor* seeks to correct Baur, Ritschl, and Harnack by drawing attention to what he calls the "classic" or "ransom" theory of the atonement. The benefit of such language is that it focuses on the main emphasis of a theologian or period and sets it in sharp contrast with the views of others, thus organizing visions held together by a central explanation of the work of Christ. The problem with "theory" language is that it simply fails to do justice to the history of the doctrine, creating unwarranted divisions, false distinctions, and interpretative biases that distort our approach to the classic theological texts of the church.

What follows is a brief overview of the history of the doctrine of the atonement that counteracts pervasive assumptions common to introductory chapters and books on this subject. The history of this doctrine is far too rich and complex for a short chapter, even a short book, on the subject. Rather, I will attempt to offer a sketch of its history that strives to accomplish three goals: (1) to provide some sense of the major contributors and shifts within the history of the doctrine, (2) to counteract some of the prevalent assumptions within comparable chapters and books on the subject, and (3) to equip the reader to profitably interact with some of the texts mentioned below. For more comprehensive treatments, I recommend the books by Oxenham, Rivière, and Franks.

Early Church: Creative Abundance

The first thousand years of the church did not see massive treatises written on the doctrine of the atonement, but from the very start we find a richly nuanced, complex, and multiaspectual understanding of the death and resurrection of Jesus. The *Epistle to Diognetus* writes of the Son's "gentleness and meekness," saving and persuading rather than using "compulsion." Compulsion "is no attribute of God," whose creative work and character are fully revealed in the re-creative work of the "beloved child," through whom we "share in his benefits and . . . see and understand." *Diognetus* describes Christ's work as a "sweet exchange" in which the Son is a ransom for us, the "holy one for the lawless, the guiltless for the guilty, the just for the unjust, the incorruptible for the corruptible, the immortal for the mortal," who "cover[s] our sins"—our "nurse, father, teacher, counselor, healer, mind, light, honor, glory, strength, and life."[10] This is just a taste of the abundance of themes woven into the early church's thinking about the work of Christ throughout the writings of the Apostolic Fathers.[11] Justin Martyr takes some of these early lines of thought, writing of the Logos, through whom God "created and set in order" all things, who "became man for our sakes, that, becoming a partaker of our sufferings, He might also bring us healing"[12]—like the Apostolic Fathers interpreting the cross in light of Isaiah 53. Justin weaves together the themes of honor and humiliation, sin-bearing, propitiation and judgment, infirmity and healing into a set of brief but conceptually rich elaborations of Christ's work thoroughly bound up with his Christology.[13]

Irenaeus, known for his doctrine of recapitulation, clearly demonstrates the riches of the early church's thinking about the work of

10. *Epistle to Diognetus* 7–9, in M. Holmes, *Apostolic Fathers in English*, 297–98.
11. Cf. *1 Clement* 7, 16, 53, 59; *2 Clement* 1, 20; Ignatius, *To the Ephesians* 9, 18–20; Ignatius, *To the Romans* 4–6; Ignatius, *To the Philadelphians* 8–9; Ignatius, *To the Smyrnaeans* 2–7, 12; Ignatius, *To Polycarp* 3; *Epistle of Barnabas* 5–7, 12–16.
12. Justin Martyr, *2 Apology* 13 (p. 84).
13. Justin Martyr, *1 Apology* 46–50 (pp. 55–58), 60–61 (pp. 65–67).

Christ. Building on Scripture's logic of recapitulation and that of
prior theologians,[14] Irenaeus responds to a range of heresies sunder-
ing the God of the Old Testament from that of the New, by arguing
that God is a good craftsman who "fitted and arranged all things by
His wisdom," through the Son "by whom all things were made," and
"in these last days, according to the time appointed by the Father,"
is "united to His own workmanship."[15] The logic of recapitulation
(developed largely across books 3–5 of *Against Heresies*) stands as a
comprehensive hermeneutic, rooted in the craftsmanship, wisdom,
and unity of God, in which God unites himself to his creation in the
person of the Son that he might fulfill his creative project. At play
are concepts of representation, propitiation of the Father, defeating
Satan, divinization, and restoring the whole of creation—a massive
and comprehensive account rooted in a rich Christology, interwoven
with the doctrine of creation[16] and summed up in the claim that "Our
Lord Jesus Christ . . . [became] what we are, that He might bring us
to be even what He is Himself."[17]

Much of this material is consolidated and advanced in one of
the most important works on the atonement from the first millennium of the church: Athanasius's *On the Incarnation of the Word*.
This short work gathers much of the insight from the early church,
revolving around a set of divine dilemmas rooted in the necessity of
God bringing his creative intentions to completion in faithfulness
to his character through the death and resurrection of the incarnate
Son, further cementing the integration of the doctrines of creation
(ex nihilo) and atonement. One of these dilemmas explores the su-
perlative consistency of the Father in upholding his law ("in the day

14. Cf. Hosea 1:2–11; Rom. 5:12–21; 1 Cor. 15:42–49; Eph. 1:3–10; *Epistle to Diognetus* 12.8–9; *Epistle of Barnabas* 3.6; 6.12–14; 15.8–9; and Justin Martyr, *Dialogue with Trypho* 100 (p. 249); 103 (p. 251); cf. *1 Apology* 67; *2 Apology* 5–6, 13.

15. Irenaeus, *Against Heresies* 2.30.9; 3.18.1 (*ANF* 1:406; 1:446).

16. Irenaeus, *Against Heresies* 3.18–25; 4.20, 22, 38; 5.1, 14–23.

17. Irenaeus, *Against Heresies* 5.preface (*ANF* 1:526). Irenaeus was the first to express what was to become a massively influential "exchange formula." Russell, "Common Christian Tradition."

that you eat of it you shall surely die" [Gen. 2:17]) and his love for his handiwork (and his honor, which is bound up with it) through the substitutionary work of the incarnate Word.[18] The doctrine of the atonement, according to Athanasius, is as rich and diverse as both the character of God and the problem of sin. God's involvement in his creation resolves a whole set of problems, which are of "such a kind and number that if anyone should wish to expound them he would be like those who gaze at the expanse of the sea and wish to count its waves."[19] The history of the doctrine of the atonement, I suggest, is a series of footnotes to the works of Irenaeus and Athanasius.

Augustine did not so much develop the doctrine as continue this fecundity of thought and promulgate it via his general influence on the church, particularly in his works *On the Trinity* (books 4 and 13), *The Enchiridion*, and *City of God* (book 10), not to mention his work on the Psalms and his sermons. In the latter works, we find many complex insights into the work of Christ, ranging from speaking of Christ as the "mousetrap" (while arguing against the idea of anything being owed to the devil) and of the "marvelous exchange"—in which Christ takes on what is ours to offer it in our place, thereby delivering us from the debt of death—to writing of the relation between Christ's deformity on the cross and our own restoration to beauty.[20]

Up to Anselm, the church demonstrates a consistent and creative interweaving of a spectrum of concepts in relation to the work of Christ across catechisms, sermons, and devotional and apologetic writings. Though theologians may have emphases, we find no such thing as a one-dimensional view or a discrete theory in the work of any one theologian or branch of the church. The goal is not to find *the explanation* for the atonement but rather to do justice to the vast array of ends accomplished by the work of God in the death and resurrection of Jesus. The works of Origen (whose view revolves around but

18. Athanasius, *On the Incarnation* 6–9 (pp. 63–69).
19. Athanasius, *On the Incarnation* 26 (p. 107).
20. Augustine, *Sermons (230–72)*, Sermon 265D, pp. 255–59. Cf. Burns, "How Christ Saves"; Meconi, *The One Christ*; Clancy, "Redemption."

transcends *Christus victor* themes), Chrysostom, Eusebius (with his interweaving of martyrdom and Christ's work), Ambrose, Ephraim of Syria, Gregory of Nyssa (with his careful account of God's justice, wisdom, power, and goodness in Christ's work, as well as his account of humanity as a single organism),[21] Leontius of Byzantium (with his account of our healing),[22] Maximos the Confessor (who explores the role of "motion" or "movement," among other things, in Jesus's passion),[23] John of Damascus,[24] Bede (throughout his commentaries), Gregory the Great, the Carolingians[25]—they all demonstrate a commitment to doing justice to the manifold nature of Christ's work in his death and resurrection, even while disagreeing on the details or emphases of their respective understandings. The first millennium of the church did not see great tomes focused specifically on the work of Christ, but it is saturated with rich and complex accounts of his work, carefully interwoven with core doctrines of the faith and central aspects of the Christian life.

The Medieval Period: Continuity and Scholasticism[26]

Two pervasive misunderstandings in works on the atonement are (1) that the emphasis on the death of Jesus as a saving event has been a Western emphasis and (2) that the doctrine of the atonement really began with Anselm's *Why God Became Man*. We have already seen these to be false, but the notion persists that a radical departure occurred through the works of Anselm and Abelard, which calls for a strong rejoinder: medieval theology relating to the atonement demonstrates a fundamental and intentional continuity with the

21. Gregory of Nyssa, *Address on Religious Instruction*, 291–312.

22. Leontius of Byzantium, *Contra Aphthartodocetas*.

23. See, for instance, questions 60–65 in Maximos, *On Difficulties in Sacred Scripture*, 427–557. Cf. Blowers, *Maximus the Confessor*, 225–53.

24. John of Damascus, *Exposition of the Orthodox Faith*.

25. Chazelle, *The Crucified God in the Carolingian Era*; Dales, *Alcuin*.

26. On the theologians of the eighth–tenth centuries preceding Anselm, see Pelikan, *Christian Tradition*, 3:106–57; Rivière, *Doctrine of the Atonement*, 2:1–13.

theologians of the early church.[27] By reading Anselm's *Prayers and Meditations*[28] and Eadmer's *Life of Anselm* in conjunction with *Why God Became Man*, this becomes amply evident. Anselm wrote his theology in self-conscious faithfulness to Augustine,[29] while demonstrating a clear emphasis on both the subjective or exemplarist and *Christus victor* themes he supposedly undermines, along with a host of other aspects of the work of Christ, all the while developing his account of satisfaction of God's honor[30] in a manner that picks up themes and commitments central to the biblical and Nicene understanding of the work of Christ.[31]

The limitations of this chapter do not allow for a full exposition, but while the rigor and focus of Anselm's work on Christ's passion, some of his key concepts, and his emphasis on a vicarious satisfactory gift to God are all to some extent developments, they are so in fundamental continuity with the tradition to which Anselm seeks to be faithful. Anselm's problem is not with the older views, those "paintings on clouds" that he himself repeats in his prayers and meditations, but with the need to take those same views and give them a stronger logical, doctrinal basis.[32] From his account of repopulating the heavenly city[33] to his argument about the rights of the devil,[34] Anselm works out a thoroughly traditional and deeply Augustinian line of thought. The same is true of Abelard, the supposed exemplarist. Reading his *Commentary on Romans* in its entirety, one finds a range

27. One of the best short introductions to medieval theologies of satisfaction remains Burns, "The Concept of Satisfaction in Medieval Redemption Theory."

28. See particularly *Prayer to Christ*, *Prayer before Receiving the Body and Blood of Christ*, *Prayer to the Holy Cross*, the three prayers to St. Mary, and *Meditation on Human Redemption* (Anselm, *Prayers and Meditations*).

29. Anselm, *Why God Became Man* 1.4 (p. 269).

30. The *Prayers* fill out the emphasis on God's honor with a host of attributes, including wisdom and justice.

31. The *Prayers* make this abundantly clear. Satisfaction, for instance, has its roots in God's care for his name—a theme resounding throughout Scripture. Cf. Anselm, "Meditation I."

32. The first chapter of Hogg's book is particularly helpful here. Hogg, *Anselm of Canterbury*.

33. Novotný, *Cur Homo?*

34. Anselm, *Why God Became Man* 2.19 (p. 354).

of ends accomplished by the death and resurrection of Christ typical of the early church, alongside an emphasis on the effect of Christ's work on the human heart and affections (not a new approach to the doctrine of the atonement at all).[35]

With Anselm and Abelard properly situated largely in continuity with the tradition preceding them, we are in a position to appreciate the continuity of medieval thought with that of its forebears while noting the difference of the scholastic method. But the spirit is the same—Thomas Aquinas's multiaspectual synthesis of the fitting work of Christ is characteristic of the era, more so even than that of Anselm's *Why God Became Man*. His manifold answer to whether there was a better way to free humankind than that of the passion of Christ, as seen in his masterful section on Christ's passion, is typical of the period.[36] Peter Lombard (who perpetuates Anselm's scholastic interaction with the tradition through his massively influential *Sentences*), William of Auvergne (with his investigation of the atonement as medicine, satisfaction, sacrifice, bath, and price, all revolving around Christ's assumption or bearing of our evils),[37] Bernard of Clairvaux (with his critique of Abelard and his account of atonement and marriage), Bonaventure, Julian of Norwich (with her devotional contemplation of the crucified Lord),[38] and Robert Grosseteste—differences abound among these theologians, but the fundamental vision is the same: to give witness to the range of ends accomplished by the work of Christ, synthesizing the works of the fathers mentioned above in a comprehensive account of the work of Christ. Nowhere is this clearer than in book 3 of Grosseteste's *On the Cessation of the Laws*, which claims that "Anselm, Augustine, and the rest of the sacred writers show most evidently that it was necessary that Christ suffer for the human race and enter into his

35. Abelard, *Commentary on the Epistle to the Romans*. Cf. Johnson, "Peter Abelard"; Lane, *Bernard of Clairvaux*, 27–40, 80–105.

36. Thomas Aquinas, *ST* III.46–52. Cf. Johnson, "A Fuller Account."

37. William of Auvergne, *Treatise on the Reasons Why God Became Man*, 29, 37.

38. Julian of Norwich, *Showings*.

glory"[39] and explains the work of Christ in terms of mediation, the restoration of all the natures of this sensible world, the overcoming of Satan, and the glorification of all creation, among other things. Such a view is incomprehensible according to modern histories of the doctrine, in which such explanations are parsed out as competing theories and in which Anselm is thought to be reacting to, rather than embracing, Augustine.

Reformation: Continuity and Narrowing of Scope

The first generation or two of Reformation theologians demonstrate great continuity with the medieval period in terms of the atonement, but for apologetic reasons, quite early on this gives way to a narrowing of scope so as to focus on the satisfaction of divine justice. Reading Luther, Zwingli, and Calvin, for instance, we see typical medieval spirit and content. Luther's *Freedom of a Christian* ranges widely, for instance, working out the atonement in terms of a marriage wherein an exchange takes place: "Christ is full of grace, life, and salvation while the soul is full of sins, death, and damnation. Now let faith enter the picture and sins, death, and damnation are Christ's while grace, life, and salvation will be the soul's. For if Christ is the bridegroom he must take upon himself that which are his bride's, and he in turn bestows on her all that is his."[40] These are concepts similar to those we find in Bernard of Clairvaux and John of the Cross, among others. Elsewhere, Luther writes of Christ's defeat of Satan—a point made popular by Gustaf Aulén—in which the Reformer stands in continuity with the early and medieval church.[41] Calvin demonstrates an even broader approach to the atoning work of Christ, working out his thought in light of Christ's office of mediator; the threefold

39. Grosseteste, *On the Cessation of the Laws*, 175.
40. Luther, *Freedom of a Christian*, 409.
41. It is a myth that only the early church believed in Christ's triumph over Satan on the cross. Nearly every work on the subject in the medieval period and many works up to the Enlightenment and beyond explore this topic at some length.

office of prophet, priest, and king; a triumphal rout of the powers of the world and air; a satisfaction of God's righteous judgment; and a fascinating account of the salvific efficacy of Christ's life as a whole, as summarized by the Apostles' Creed.[42] We find much the same diversity in Vermigli, Zwingli, and Hooker.[43]

Within a short time, however, Protestant theology took a distinctive turn within the history of the doctrine, decidedly narrowing its focus on the doctrine of satisfaction, with a particular emphasis on divine justice. The reasons for this seem to be largely apologetic: On the one hand, satisfaction of divine justice provided the soteriological foundation for the doctrine of justification by faith, a key emphasis of the Reformation. On the other hand, the Lutheran defense against Osiander, together with the Reformed defense against the critiques of Socinus's *De Jesu Christu servatore* (which argues that God did not need or desire satisfaction of his justice in order to forgive sin), led to a further entrenchment in this emphasis.[44] The Reformed scholastics (cf. Turretin[45] and Heppe[46]) and Lutheran scholastics tend to stay fairly narrowly focused on the doctrine of penal satisfaction.[47] See, for instance, Owen and Baxter's debate over the nature of satisfaction, with the thought of Grotius and Socinus looming in the background.[48]

That said, however, the old patterns of thinking persisted. Jonathan Edwards, for instance, follows Turretin in much of his thinking, but his sermon "The Wisdom of God Displayed in the Way of Salvation" covers a host of aspects of the saving work of Christ, from Satan and

---

42. Calvin, *Institutes* II.xii–xvii (pp. 464–534). Cf. R. A. Peterson, *Calvin and the Atonement*; Jones, "Fury of Love."

43. Vermigli, *Early Writings*, 32–50; Zwingli, *On Providence*, 241–47; Hooker, *Of the Laws of Ecclesiastical Polity*, 2:201–40.

44. Melanchthon, for instance, organizes his account of the work of Christ in *Loci Communes*, a work approved by Luther, though it lacks the breadth of his thought regarding the atonement.

45. Turretin, *Institutes of Elenctic Theology*, vol. 2.

46. Heppe, *Reformed Dogmatics*.

47. Discussions on the extent of the atonement, motivated in part by Amyraldism, further perpetuated this emphasis. See Bird and Harrower, *Unlimited Atonement*.

48. Tay, "Christ's Priestly Oblation and Intercession."

the angels to the full spectrum of divine attributes, suggesting that the change in Protestant theology was not so much one of belief as one of emphasis and perceived polemic need. The poems of George Herbert ("The Sacrifice" stands preeminently among them)[49] and John Donne,[50] Charles Wesley's hymns,[51] Thomas Traherne's meditations (particularly on the grounds of the doctrine of satisfaction within God's own being and life),[52] and John Milton's reflections on Christ's work in *Paradise Lost* and *Paradise Regained* provide more grounds for thinking that the Protestant emphasis on the satisfaction of divine justice was a material commitment shared with the early and medieval church, but with a unique emphasis. When worshiping or writing in a nonpolemical way, the Protestants were as broad in scope as their ancient and medieval forebears, but they were far narrower in their apologetic or polemic writings.[53]

Modern Theology

Following Enlightenment critiques of traditional doctrines, the nineteenth century brought a significant change of scope to Protestant

49. Other than "The Sacrifice," see especially his poems "Affliction," "Prayer (2)," "The Drawing," "Business," "Justice," "The Bag," "Clasping of Hands," "Mary Magdalene," "Discipline," and "Judgment."

50. See especially his poems "The Cross," "Upon the Annunciation and Passion Falling upon One Day," "A Litany," "La Corona," and "A Hymn to Christ, at the Author's Last Going into Germany."

51. Chilcote, *Faith That Sings*, 15–29.

52. Traherne, *Centuries of Meditations*. See especially meditations 41–44, 54–64, from "The First Century."

53. It is worth noting a trend in contemporary studies of the atonement: the retrieval of the doctrine of divinization, theosis, or deification as a major topic of study. This was once thought to be a primarily Eastern emphasis, found in the writings of Irenaeus, Athanasius, and other Orthodox theologians. Recently, however, a host of works have highlighted the role of divinization in Western theology, including in Tertullian, Ambrose, Augustine, Thomas Aquinas, Luther, Calvin, and Wesley, to name but a few. Cf. Christensen and Wittung, *Partakers of the Divine Nature*; Kharlamov, *Theosis*; Louth, "Place of *Theosis* in Orthodox Theology"; McCormack, "Participation in God, Yes; Deification, No"; McGuckin, "Strategic Adaptation of Deification in the Cappadocians"; Meconi, *The One Christ*; Russell, *The Doctrine of Deification in the Greek Patristic Tradition*; Meconi and Olson, *Called to Be Children of God*; Ortiz, *Deification in the Latin Patristic Tradition*; Kimbrough, *Lyrical Theology of Charles Wesley*.

theology.[54] A common goal in that era was to formulate an account of Christ's work that was not merely exemplarist (Ritschl, for instance, critiqued Schleiermacher for this failure) but also free from what were perceived to be decisive critiques of traditional views of the atonement. Kant's critique of vicarious satisfaction is one such attempt: his alternative is to posit the incarnate Son of God as the personification of the act of conversion, in which we become new moral beings.[55] Hegel's approach in his last cycle of the *Lectures on the Philosophy of Religion* is to suggest that Jesus's taking upon himself the evil of humanity so as to destroy it by his death is a moment in the life of God: "*God has died, God is dead*," but "he maintains himself in this process, and the latter is only the death of death. God rises again to life" and so overcomes finitude in all its forms.[56] This emphasis on the suffering of God via the incarnation was to play a significant role in the twentieth century in varying degrees in the thought of Karl Barth, Hans Urs von Balthasar, Jürgen Moltmann, and Kazoh Kitamori.

Schleiermacher's account of theology, rooted in the sense of absolute dependence, formulated a "mystical" account of redemption in which "the redeemer takes up persons of faith into the strength of his God-consciousness."[57] In Ritschl and Harnack, we have a further emphasis on the forgiveness we experience in Christ—an intentional movement away from traditional accounts. As Harnack puts it, the work of Christ causes "their [sinners'] terror of the awful judge [to melt] away, and they believe that the Holy One is Love, and that *there is something mightier still than Justice—Mercy* . . . ; [His death] had the single object of convincing sinners that forgiving Love is mightier than the Justice before which they tremble."[58] We cannot "measure and register" what Christ did, but we can "in our turn feel it for ourselves

---

54. Exemplarism, or the moral theory of the atonement—often argued to originate with Abelard—is rather the product of the Enlightenment. McGrath, "Moral Theory of the Atonement."

55. Kant, *Religion within the Boundaries of Mere Reason*, 84–93.

56. Hegel, *Lectures on the Philosophy of Religion*, 465–66n199 (emphasis original).

57. Schleiermacher, *Christian Faith*, §100, p. 621.

58. Harnack, "Atonement," 18–19 (emphasis original).

with the same freedom with which it was originally felt"[59]—when we feel what ought to have come upon us by seeing Christ's suffering and when, through this awareness, we are both shamed and purified.

As the nineteenth century progressed, German influence brought a renewed breadth to the doctrine, with theologians canvassing a wider range of views or theories of the doctrine, though for the most part the emphasis remained rather one-dimensional. Hodge,[60] Dorner,[61] and Miley,[62] for instance, argue for the satisfaction of divine justice, though Miley does so in a governmental manner (following Grotius), while Hodge affirms "a real satisfaction of divine justice, . . . real substitution, and . . . [a] real enduring of the penalty of the law."[63] Dorner proceeds along similar lines.

The propensity to hold on to a central commitment (such as penal substitution) often coincided with a broader commitment more typical of the early and medieval church. The growing historical consciousness of the church, stemming from the likes of Baur, Ritschl, and Harnack, combined with Catholic *ressourcement* and growing theologies of retrieval in other branches of the church,[64] led to a proliferation of studies in the twentieth and twenty-first centuries relating to different aspects of the atonement. We now have translated works and extensive bibliographies relating to the atonement theologies of most of the key figures in the history of the doctrine— something virtually inconceivable prior to the nineteenth century.

Contemporary Questions and Trajectories

Contemporary work on the doctrine of the atonement is wideranging, but a case could be made that current discussions revolve around several key questions. First, what is the role of suffering in

59. Harnack, *What Is Christianity?*, 160.
60. Hodge, *Systematic Theology*, 2:455–591.
61. Dorner, *System of Christian Doctrine*, 4:1–126.
62. Miley, *Atonement in Christ*.
63. Hodge, *Systematic Theology*, 2:573.
64. Sarisky, *Theologies of Retrieval*; Webster, "Theologies of Retrieval."

the divine life, through the incarnation and passion of the Son of God? There is a growing interest in the role of suffering in the divine life, partly through the significant influence of Barth, Balthasar, and Moltmann and partly through the influence of feminist and womanist theology. This conversation often revolves around divine impassibility[65] and the theology of Holy Saturday.[66] Second, is there a significant negative aspect to God's purpose for the cross? Specifically, is the death of Jesus in any sense an act of judgment or wrath on the part of God? Two aspects of this discussion are central: (1) whether and in what way the sin of humankind is taken up by the incarnate Son; and (2) how the Bible and theology account for wrath, holiness, and justice (particularly as the latter two relate to sin). Third, what is the role of divine revelation within the doctrine? Are we at liberty to formulate our own understandings of the doctrine? Are the experiences of minority groups and cultures (e.g., women, African Americans, inmates, those with disabilities) normative for shaping theological commitments, do they open interpretative possibilities, or do they play a less substantial role in the formation of theological judgments, positing questions and providing illustrations? Fourth, how are the various aspects of the atonement united? Most works on the doctrine espouse a plurality of images, metaphors, aspects, or theories. How are these related to each other? Are they the products of different languages and cultures, stages of thought development, part of a hierarchy in which one of them explains the others? And fifth, what is the extent of the atonement? A rising interest in universalism is clearly evident in the literature.[67]

Conclusion: A Guide for Further Study

Much like the previous chapter on Holy Scripture, this chapter is not meant to be comprehensive; it provides little more than an overview

---

65. Keating and White, *Divine Impassibility*.
66. Balthasar, *Mysterium Paschale*; A. Lewis, *Between Cross and Resurrection*.
67. Cf. McClymond, *The Devil's Redemption*.

of the history of the doctrine and some of its key developments. Neither is the chapter meant to supply a conclusive argument; it provides, rather, a number of theses meant to correct errors typical of introductory chapters (and books) to equip the reader to delve into some of these works for themselves. In this conclusion, I will draw attention to some of these theses, with the hope of facilitating further work on the subject.

First, I contend that chapters and books on the history of the doctrine of the atonement are a modern development, rooted in the thought of Schleiermacher, Baur, and Ritschl. And this heritage has come with a bias—an inclination to emphasize development through contrasts and conflicts, which supposedly culminate in the insights of nineteenth-century theology. The challenge is to study the history of the doctrine but to do so in a way that attends to the unity of that witness as much as to its disagreements, as well as to refuse to posit conflict where there is mere difference. Much (though not all!) of the supposed divergence throughout the history of the doctrine rises from the misguided attempt to find a single distinctive feature of a theologian's account of Christ's passion, so as to set it apart from that of their fellows or theologians of other periods—an attempt inherently foreign to how these theologians approached the doctrine. An equally great source of misunderstanding, which is directly connected to the first, lies in emphasizing genuine difference or disagreement at the expense of acknowledging equally important agreements.

Second, many of the theologians above have exceptionally rich views of the doctrine that include a whole range of explanations for the necessity or fittingness of Christ's atonement. When I wrote, for instance, of "Leontius of Byzantium (with his account of our healing)," that was meant to be a gesture toward an interesting aspect of his account, which includes far more than this aspect; it was not intended to summarize or note the organizing principle of his thought. Actions often have multiple motivations and many consequences. Nowhere is this truer than in discussions of the death and resurrection of Jesus. Our goal when reading Dante, Athanasius, or Justin

Martyr is to be guided by them, as far as possible, in understanding the work of Christ in all its complexity.

Third, we ought to be as attentive as we are able to the presuppositions, questions, and categories we bring to the interpretative task. "Which 'theory' of the atonement did Maximos hold?" one might ask. As it turns out, he predates such a concept by over one thousand years, and he would be fundamentally opposed to this notion. "What was Athanasius's doctrine of the 'atonement'?" The word didn't exist in the fourth century, even in Greek. "Did Anselm argue for or against 'penal substitution'?" The term didn't exist even in the twelfth century; in fact, the first few generations of Reformers spoke of the doctrine of satisfaction. This is not to say the concept didn't exist, but we must be careful to not overlook the emphases, concerns, and views of those we seek to interpret because of the terms and concepts we use (or for any other reason, for that matter). "Is view *x* more 'Eastern' or 'Western'?" Here, too, we must be cautious. Thomas Aquinas cites an equal number of Western and Eastern authorities in his account of Christ's passion in the *Summa Theologica*, and though he cites Augustine more than anyone, the next most frequent references are to Athanasius and John of Damascus, who are treated as authorities.[68]

What to do from here? One step would be to read other, more detailed, histories of the doctrine—particularly those by Franks, Oxenham, and Rivière—and to read secondary sources on the thought of different figures on the work of Christ, by specialists on those figures. But nothing replaces reading the primary sources themselves.[69] For those interested in further study of the doctrine of the atonement, particularly its history, my recommendation is to (a) cultivate patience[70] and (b) choose one figure and either read everything they wrote (if possible) or read widely from their works (i.e., read whole books rather than selections wherever possible), including a range

68. Dauphinais, Hofer, and Nutt, *Thomas Aquinas and the Greek Fathers*.
69. Webster, *Culture of Theology*, 45.
70. Webster, "Intellectual Patience."

of genres (e.g., treatises, commentaries, sermons, letters, devotional writings) and writings from various periods of their life—not just works that pertain to the death and resurrection of Jesus. Doing so brings out nuances and other perspectives that complement their treatment of the atonement in works devoted to that subject, providing a well-rounded view of the subject. And after one has done that, I recommend doing the same thing with another theologian or two from roughly the same time period, allowing continuities, differences, and nuances to emerge in the process. This sort of primary text work provides the basis for a far more fruitful interaction with secondary sources on the subject and histories of the doctrine.

But the goal here is not simply mastery of the history or something of the sort; it is to be guided, as far as possible, by our mothers and fathers in the faith who have gone before us in interpreting Scripture, to better understand the work of Christ for us and for our salvation. The goal, as always, is an exercise in faith seeking understanding—an act of worship and of personal and corporate formation, as we are built up by the Spirit into the body of Christ, being remade in his image.

DOXOLOGICAL INTERLUDE

John Donne's "Holy Sonnet 10"

Death, be not proud, though some have called thee
Mighty and dreadful, for thou are not so;
For those whom thou think'st thou dost overthrow
Die not, poor Death, nor yet canst thou kill me.
From rest and sleep, which but thy pictures be,
Much pleasure; then from thee much more must flow,
And soonest our best men with thee do go,
Rest of their bones, and soul's delivery.
Thou'art slave to fate, chance, kings, and desperate men,
And dost with poison, war, and sickness dwell,
And poppy'or charms can make us sleep as well
And better than thy stroke; why swell'st thou then?
One short sleep past, we wake eternally,
And death shall be no more; Death, thou shalt die.[1]

1. See https://poets.org/poem/death-be-not-proud-holy-sonnet-10.

CHAPTER FOUR

The Spirit of Atonement

The Role of the Holy Spirit in Christ's Death and Resurrection

WRITTEN WITH TESSA HAYASHIDA

THIS CHAPTER BUILDS on the book's emphasis on worship and the third article of the Apostles' Creed, seeking to develop a constructive proposal for what I take to be one of the more neglected aspects of the doctrine of the atonement: the role of the Holy Spirit in the death and resurrection of Jesus. Gregory of Nazianzus writes:

> Christ is born, the Spirit is his forerunner; Christ is baptized, the Spirit bears him witness; Christ is tempted, the Spirit leads him up; Christ performs miracles, the Spirit accompanies him; Christ ascends, the Spirit fills his place. Is there any significant function belonging to God, which the Spirit does not perform?[1]

This chapter is a modified version of an article cowritten by Adam Johnson and Tessa Hayashida, "The Spirit of the Atonement: The Role of the Holy Spirit in Christ's Death and Resurrection," *Religions* 13, no. 10 (2022), https://doi.org/10.3390/rel13100918.

1. Gregory of Nazianzus, *On God and Christ*, 139.

Indeed, there is not; as Augustine says, "The Holy Spirit . . . is in no way excluded from the activity of the Father and the Son."[2] But skipping from Christ's miracles to his ascension is disappointingly representative of the tradition, which offers relatively scant reflection on this lacuna—an omission likely due to Scripture itself having little to say beyond the fact that it was "through the eternal Spirit" that Christ "offered himself without blemish to God" (Heb. 9:14).[3] For the sake of consistency and the enrichment of the doctrine, it is both fitting and pious that we seek to account for the role and activity of the Spirit in Christ's saving work, for surely we must envisage the Spirit "as having as full a place in the divine economy of salvation as the other persons."[4] We believe in and worship the Holy Spirit as fully God; we worship the one God who is fully present and active in all his works; and therefore we can and should delight in understanding the role of the Spirit in the death and resurrection of Jesus, both for us and for our salvation.

In this chapter, we marshal resources from a range of biblical, trinitarian, and soteriological commitments to offer a doctrinal proposal for the Spirit's role in the triune God's work of at-one-ment. We argue that the Spirit plays a vital role in the atoning work of the triune God, as the Spirit is the love of God directed toward the incarnate Son in a twofold manner: (1) *in the mode of wrath* against our sin, borne by Christ our representative, and (2) *in the mode of blessing* the resurrected and ascended Christ, the exalted one in whom we receive the promised Holy Spirit.[5] Seen in this light,

2. Augustine, *Sermons (51–94)*, Sermon 52, p. 52. Cf. Vidu, *The Same God Who Works All Things*.

3. "Jonathan Edwards complained that the atonement theology he had received pictured the Spirit merely as the one who applied the benefits of the atoning transaction between Father and Son, which he believed did undervalue the divine personhood of the Spirit. His solution was to propose that the gift given to the redeemed in the atonement was not merely Christ's righteousness, but the person of the Spirit" (S. Holmes, "Penal Substitution," 300). Perhaps this omission is due to larger patterns of pneumatology within the church. Castelo, "Holy Spirit," 103–4.

4. Webster, "Identity of the Holy Spirit," 6.

5. This chapter develops some of the main theological commitments found in Frank Macchia's delightful and wide-ranging chapter on the subject, which we read when doing the final edits on this project. Macchia, *Jesus the Spirit Baptizer*, 247–300.

Christ's death and resurrection are God's twofold act of love in the Spirit—the twofold means of making our representative, Jesus, a fit receptacle for the promised Holy Spirit, that in him all the peoples of the earth might be blessed through his recapitulation of Israel's relationship to the Spirit. Key to this thesis are two commitments: (1) seeing a changing economic relationship between Jesus and the Holy Spirit, integral to Jesus's recapitulation of Israel, and (2) viewing wrath as a mode of God's love and therefore as a part of, rather than something alien to, the work of the Spirit. With these doctrinal resources in hand, we have the necessary conceptual tools to affirm, in a tentative yet confident way, that the Spirit, just as much as the Father and the Son, is the one who saves us in the death and resurrection of Jesus.

The Background: Trinity and Representation

Atonement and monotheism go hand in hand, for this is the work not of three gods but of the one God, who in and of himself and from eternity is who he is as Father, Son, and Holy Spirit. The acts of God reiterate the fundamental reality of God's oneness: they are the single, variegated act of Father, Son, and Holy Spirit, "for the holy and blessed Triad is indivisible and one in itself. When mention is made of the Father, there is included also his Word, and the Spirit who is in the Son."[6] The works of God are undivided: "opera trinitatis ad extra indivisa sunt."[7] Fully God, the Son is eternally one with both the Father and the Holy Spirit, a claim true both of the immanent life of God and of God's economic acts, including the incarnation: "The Father was present by approving the incarnation, while the Holy Spirit cooperated with the Son who carried it out."[8]

---

6. Athanasius, *Letters concerning the Holy Spirit*, 94.

7. Vidu, *The Same God Who Works All Things*.

8. Maximos, *Expositio orationis dominicae* (CCSG 23:31–32, lines 87–89), cited in Blowers, *Maximus the Confessor*, 147.

The challenge of the atonement in relation to the Spirit is to give an account of Christ's progressive and seemingly changing relationship to the Spirit and the Father in the course of his passion. For that which we easily affirm of the immanent Trinity (its undivided unity) is far more difficult to affirm in the life of Christ, where the Father's statement "This is my beloved Son, with whom I am well pleased" (Matt. 3:17) becomes his silence in response to the Son's request "If it be possible, let this cup pass" (26:39); in fact, the Father's assertion ultimately becomes the far more dramatic silence to Jesus's cry "My God, my God, why have you forsaken me?" (27:46). From speech to silence and even unbearable silence: How do we account for this change? One possibility is to favor a more social model of the Trinity, allowing for rupture, division, or separation between Father, Son, and Holy Spirit, such as one finds in Moltmann.[9] Against such a position, we explore the trinitarian implications of Christ's representative sin-bearing, which introduces a new dynamic to the relationship between Father, incarnate Son, and Spirit, a dynamic that must be overcome by God himself—as, to revise Athanasius's famous statement, God makes our sin his own, that the unity which is properly his might be ours (John 17).[10]

9. We do not here develop our rejection of this position, which one finds in Moltmann, *Crucified God* (see also A. Lewis, *Between Cross and Resurrection*, 324–25). Moltmann, for instance, writes, "The abandonment on the cross which separates the Son from the Father is something which takes place within God himself; it is *stasis* within God—'God against God.' . . . The cross of the Son divides God from God to the utmost degree of enmity and distinction. The resurrection of the Son abandoned by God unites God with God in the most intimate fellowship" (Moltmann, *Crucified God*, 151–52; cf. 241–47, 272–78). A constitutive problem with this view is that it makes the life of Jesus immanent, speaking of the relationship between the Father and the Son on the cross—but "neither God alone does this, nor man alone, but God as man"—a fact that profoundly shapes the claims we make about opposition and the life of God (Wynne, *Wrath among the Perfections of God's Life*, 170). Essentially, since the differentiation of the Father, Son, and Holy Spirit lies not in different substances, personalities, or characteristics but in modes of relation alone (Anselm, "On the Procession of the Holy Spirit," 392), there is no room for the kind of relationality posited within a social model, such as conflict, rupture, or disunity. "The work of the Father is not separate or distinct from the work of the Son; whatever the Son 'sees the Father doing . . . that the Son does likewise'" (Basil, *On the Holy Spirit*, 39; cf. 40). On this subject, see McCall, *Forsaken*, 13–47.
10. Athanasius, *On the Incarnation* 54 (p. 167). Cf. Maximos, *On Difficulties in the Church Fathers*, 1:37 (Ambigua 5); Balthasar, *Theo-Drama*, 4:362.

At the heart of this thesis is Jesus's identity as our representative: what happens to him happens to us, for we (the baptized) are in him.[11] Along these lines, Paul writes that he died and was raised in Christ (Gal. 2:20; Col. 3:1). But lest we take this individualistically, Jesus is the representative of Israel, the one in whom the history of Israel is taken up, repeated, and fulfilled.[12] Jesus, while fully man, fully individual, is simultaneously more than that: he is the representative of Israel. Jesus "accepts personal responsibility for all the unfaithfulness, the deceit, the rebellion of this people and its priests and kings." Jesus is the "one Israelite," the one who "made Himself the object of this accusation and willed to confess Himself a sinner, and to be regarded as such."[13] Jesus is the representative of Israel, the Israelite in whom the history of his people is repeated in all its suffering and judgment, and the one in whom all its promises are fulfilled.

But to affirm Jesus as the representative of Israel in whom God takes to himself the curse of God's chosen but rebellious people, that in him they might receive the fullness of God's blessings and promises[14]—that is a powerful but still generic statement. For what was the curse that God took upon himself in Jesus, and what were the blessings which he sought to share? And how do the answers to these questions help us connect the work of the Spirit to the doctrine of the atonement?

The Holy Spirit: The Curse and the Blessing

The curse and blessing of Israel are inseparable from the person and work of the Holy Spirit. It was the Spirit who hovered over the waters of creation (Gen. 1:2); who led the exodus of Israel, bringing them to their rest and instructing them (Isa. 63:11–14; Neh. 9:20); and who set apart judges, prophets, and kings (Num. 11:16–25; Judg. 3:10;

11. Cf. Johnson, "Barth and Boethius on *Stellvertretung* and Personhood"; Graham, "Substitution and Representation"; Crisp, *Participation and Atonement*.

12. Leithart, *Delivered from the Elements of the World*, 200.

13. Barth, *CD* IV/1, 172. Cf. N. T. Wright, *Paul and the Faithfulness of God*, 2:828.

14. This is a rendition of Athanasius's axiom in a corporate, Israelite key.

6:34; 11:29; 14:6, 19; 1 Sam. 10:6–7; 11:1–11). And it was Israel's great hope that it would receive the Spirit in a lavish form at some point in its future. Isaiah and Joel tell of a time when God will pour out the Holy Spirit on Israel's offspring (Isa. 44:3) and all people (Joel 2:28–32), and Ezekiel writes of God's promise to "give you a new heart and put a new spirit in you" (Ezek. 36:26 NIV), concluding his great vision of the valley of dry bones with God's promise: "I will put my Spirit in you and you will live, and I will settle you in your own land" (37:14 NIV). This is a corporate matter, for the fate of Israel is the fate of a people, at the center of which is the Spirit-filled tabernacle—the place consecrated for the presence and glory of the Lord, at the center of the life and liturgy of Israel.

The Spirit of the Lord, the blessed presence of God's glory among God's people and temple, is no optional addition, no "bonus" for creaturely existence. Rather, the presence or indwelling of the Spirit is the aim and goal of creation, its perfection and completion. Life in its fullness *is* life in the Spirit. When the Spirit departs, creation reverts to what it was—dust and chaos (Gen. 6:3; Ps. 104:29–30; Eccles. 12:7).[15] To be human is to be called to be the people of God, and to be such is to be a people indwelled by the Holy Spirit. The New Testament draws on the Old Testament vision, affirming that we "are God's temple and that God's Spirit dwells in [us]" (1 Cor. 3:16). This is the aim of creation, its proper end, as bestowed by its creator. Fallen creation, nothing but a valley of dry bones, longs for the breath of the Lord, for God to put the Holy Spirit within us (Ezek. 37:1–14).

The withdrawal of the Spirit, whether from the individual, the people, or the temple or tabernacle, is not a return to a state of neutrality or balance but an act of judgment on the part of God.[16] "The Holy Spirit is not a harmless dove" but "the sovereign God. He brings judgment through the history of revelation."[17] The Lord washes away

---

15. C. J. H. Wright, *Knowing the Holy Spirit through the Old Testament*, 29.

16. On the dialectic of presence and withdrawal in the Spirit's act of judgment, see Tan, *The Spirit at the Cross*, 248–49.

17. Horton, *Rediscovering the Holy Spirit*, 177.

the filth of the daughters of Zion by a "spirit of judgment and by a
spirit of burning" (Isa. 4:4). The Spirit of God "brings the impact of
his divine power and holiness to bear directly and personally upon
their lives in judgment and salvation alike,"[18] and he witnesses both in
their defense and against them.[19] Because the Spirit's blessing is God's
telos for creation, removing such blessing is a curse, an act of judgment.
Before the creator God, our alternative is not between generic life and
blessing but between life and death, blessings and curses (Deut. 30:19).
God's rejection of Saul is the Spirit's work: "The Spirit of the LORD
had departed from Saul, and an evil spirit from the LORD tormented
him" (1 Sam. 16:14 NIV). Much the same happens in the judgment
and rejection of Israel, as Ezekiel chronicles the gradual departure of
the glory of God from the temple, synonymous with the departure of
the Spirit (Ezek. 9:3; 10:4, 18, 19; 11:23)—leaving the temple desolate
and the people scattered among the nations.[20] The psalmist knows
that to experience the absence of God's Spirit is to sink into the pit,
into Sheol; departure is an act of judgment, a way of speaking of the
removal of the blessings of the Spirit. More generally, Scripture uses
the distinctive characteristics of the Spirit, breath and fire, to speak of
the Spirit's work of judgment, binding judgment closely to the being
and work of the Spirit.[21] In short, the Spirit is the vehicle of both God's

18. Torrance, *Trinitarian Faith*, 192.
19. Horton, *Rediscovering the Holy Spirit*, 109.
20. Block, *Book of Ezekiel*, 1:326.
21. The sign of the Spirit at Pentecost is tongues of fire (Acts 2:1–4)—imagery drawn from the Old Testament, where the presence and glory of the Lord is bound up with the imagery of fire (Exod. 3:2; 40:38). The Lord himself is described as "a consuming fire, a jealous God" (Deut. 4:24; cf. 9:1–5), whose "love is strong as death, / jealousy is fierce as the grave. / Its flashes are flashes of fire, / the very flame of the LORD" (Song 8:6). The people had to purify themselves and maintain proper distance, lest the fire of the Lord burn among them and consume them (Num. 11:1–3). The New Testament likewise speaks of God as "a consuming fire" (Heb. 12:29).
At its extreme, this fire is the sign of God's judgment and punishment (Gen. 19:24–26; Josh. 7:15). To be in the presence of God, items (and people) had to be clean, and one of the chief means of accomplishing this was fire, which would destroy impurities while purifying the object (Num. 31:21–24). This purification continues on into the New Testament, where the Spirit is associated with fire and judgment (Matt. 3:11–12). As Macchia puts it,

blessing and God's curse, and ultimately there is no neutral ground between these two, before the maker of heaven and earth.

To this biblical evidence for the Spirit's role in judgment, we add a systematic insight. The conjunction of the Spirit and love is a powerful and pervasive one in discourse on the Trinity,[22] taking its shape from the economy of God's acts (i.e., it is through the Spirit that God's love is poured out into our hearts [Rom. 5:5]). And this insight provides powerful support for the role of the Spirit in the wrath of God,[23] for wrath is not a distinct attribute in the life of God—God is not a God of eternal wrath, and wrath does not shape and characterize the immanent life of God as Father, Son, and Holy Spirit. Rather, wrath "belongs to [God's] perfection as a mode" of God's love against sin and opposition.[24] Barth writes of God's love as pure and therefore as resisting and judging sin:

> In Him, of course, there is no sin which He has first to resist. But . . .
> He is Himself the purity, which as such contradicts and will resist

---

"In bearing the Spirit for humanity, Christ bears also the fire of judgment." Macchia, *Jesus the Spirit Baptizer*, 251.

Jesus shares his Spirit with his disciples by breathing on them (John 20:22), but it is likewise by breath (*ruakh* or *pneuma*) that God or Jesus exercises judgment (2 Sam. 22:16; cf. Ps. 18:15). Isaiah weaves together breath and fire in speaking of judgment (Isa. 30:33; cf. 40:7), noting that Jacob was judged by the "fierce breath" of God (27:7–9). Second Thessalonians picks up on this theme, claiming that Jesus will overthrow the lawless one "with the breath of his mouth" (2:8). Cf. Tan, *The Spirit at the Cross*, 178, 255–73.

22. Thomas Aquinas, for instance, writes that "besides the procession of the Word in God, there exists in Him another procession called the procession of love," referring to the Spirit (*ST* I.27.23; cf. I.37). Of course, Western theology is not unique in affirming the relationship between the Spirit and the love of God; we make the point here in a Thomistic vein, which could be reworked in a manner more fitting for Eastern theology.

23. For wrath is the wrath of God, not of the Father per se (McCall, *Forsaken*, 45–46, 79–86). "When we refer to the Father alone or the Son alone, we understand nothing . . . other than the same and only true God that we know when we mention each one"—a point as true of wrath as it is of anything else other than "the relation whereby they are related to one another" (Anselm, "On the Procession of the Holy Spirit," 405; cf. 434).

24. Wynne, *Wrath among the Perfections of God's Life*, 173. In a similar vein, Moltmann writes that wrath "is injured love and therefore a mode of [God's] reaction to men. Love is the source and the basis of the possibility of the wrath of God" (*Crucified God*, 272). Cf. Balthasar, *Theo-Drama*, 4:338–51; Lane, "The Wrath of God as an Aspect of the Love of God."

everything which is unlike itself, yet which does not evade this opposing factor, but, because it is the purity of the life of the Father, Son
and Holy Spirit, eternally reacts against it, resisting and judging it in
its encounter with it, but in so doing receiving and adopting it, and
thus entering into the fellowship with it which redeems it.[25]

The love of God is a holy and pure love. In himself, as Father, Son,
and Holy Spirit, there is no sin, no contradiction, nothing to resist.
The holy purity of the love of God is, as such, simply the life of God.
But this purity of God's love "contradicts and will resist everything
which is unlike [or opposed to] itself," which "eternally reacts against
it, resisting and judging it in its encounter with it." And it is this new
dynamic of opposition or resistance that we refer to when we use the
language of modality.

The attributes of God—or perfections, as Barth calls them—are
"modes" of the divine being.[26] But they can and do take on a further
mode of activity in the presence of sin, where the purity of the life of
God opposes that which is opposed to it, not because God is changing from being loving to being wrathful but because the creature is
changing and opposing him. By our sin, we call forth what is variously
known as a mode, aspect, form, dimension, or characteristic of the
character and perfection of God that is not experienced as such in the
eternal life of the Trinity, given the lack of opposition or negation. But
this is not just relative to us and our experience; wrath is not merely
in the eye of the sinner. God's "wrath is his response to something
outside of himself," for the "holy, loving God acts differently toward
us in different circumstances"[27]—not that God acts inconsistently
or is at odds with himself. Rather, as the living and active God, God
extends himself and therefore his character toward the creature in a
manner fitting to its condition. Divine wrath is the exercise of divine
love toward the sinful creature (for "His wrath is not separate from

25. Barth, *CD* II/1, 368.
26. Barth, *CD* II/1, 353.
27. Lane, "The Wrath of God as an Aspect of the Love of God," 146, 163.

but in His love").[28] But it is the exercise of a love that must oppose that which it seeks to embrace, for the beloved is deeply opposed to God. "Binding Israel to Himself, He becomes to it the inextinguishable fire whose flame is nothing else but the flame of His love"—a love that first must consume in order to subsequently restore.[29] The becoming here signifies not a change in the character or will of God but a condition permeating Israel, calling forth the love of God in its oppositional mode, the character of God extended toward God's sinful people.

For this reason, love and wrath do not need to be balanced in God; the problem is sin, not the balance of love and wrath within the divine life.[30] But if the Spirit is the love of the Father and the Son, and if wrath is a mode of love, then it follows that the Spirit is likewise the wrath of the Father and the Son—their love in the face of sin. The Spirit must be an essential part of a fully trinitarian account of both wrath and the atonement.

The Spirit and Christ, Part 1: A Changing Relationship

How, then, does Jesus recapitulate Israel's relationship with the Spirit of God?[31] To set the stage for an answer, we begin with Luke's nuanced relationship between Jesus and the Spirit: the two baptisms of Jesus (Luke 3:21; 12:50), paired with his twofold receiving of the Spirit (Luke 3:22; Acts 2:33).[32] "The Holy Spirit," the same being true of the eternal Son, "being in God, must be incapable of change, variation, and corruption."[33] The new dynamic in the relation between the incarnate Son and the Spirit is not a "change" in the Spirit or the Son,

---

28. Barth, *CD* II/1, 363.
29. Barth, *CD* II/1, 367.
30. Moltmann, *Crucified God*, 272.
31. Tan, *The Spirit at the Cross*, 255.
32. Luke is in some ways an unlikely place to ground the integration of atonement and the Holy Spirit, for "several interpreters argue that Luke simply has little or no sense of the cross as a salvific event." Moffitt, *Rethinking the Atonement*, 241.
33. Athanasius, *Letters concerning the Holy Spirit*, 130.

for "what the Spirit does among us is repeat or reiterate the Spirit's acts within the eternal life of God."[34] But it can be a new mode of relating within the same fundamental dynamic: the same relationship; the enactment of the same divine character or attributes in a new mode, determined by the human nature taken on by the eternal Son in the incarnation; and the sin-bearing this entails.[35]

Luke records that "the Holy Spirit descended on him in bodily form, like a dove; and a voice came from heaven, 'You are my beloved Son; with you I am well pleased'" (Luke 3:22), to which the Gospel of John adds, "and it remained on him" (John 1:32). Though the divine Son is in full participation with the Father and Spirit, here in the "descending" and "remaining" Jesus relates to the Spirit in a new but potentially ambiguous way. Was this the inauguration of the Spirit's permanent and salvific indwelling (akin to that of Pentecost for the disciples), or was it an experience in keeping with the Spirit's coming upon different Israelites throughout the Old Testament?[36] Dunn advocates that "what Jordan was to Jesus, Pentecost was to the disciples,"[37] but such a view encroaches upon the new reality initiated through Christ's death and resurrection, prematurely drawing the incarnate Son into a participation in new creation prior to his elevation as the firstborn of creation (Col. 1:18). Dunn's interpretation

34. C. R. J. Holmes, "The Atonement and the Holy Spirit," 79.

35. As Tanner puts it, "Because Jesus already has the Spirit for his own insofar as he is divine, it is his humanity that is at issue in his coming to have the Spirit in a particular point in his life" (*Christ the Key*, 167). To be fair, she makes this a matter more of the Spirit's evidence in Jesus's life than his objective presence (*Christ the Key*, 168). She does, however, speak of the way that "the human world of sin and death into which the persons of the trinity enter should . . . make some difference to their relations with one another. . . . Not everything . . . about the relations among the persons of the trinity in their mission for us also holds for their relations simply among themselves" (*Christ the Key*, 180).

One of the strongest proponents for a changing or progressing relationship between Jesus and the Spirit is Bulgakov, *The Comforter*, 245–66. "The eternal, inseparable, and inconfusible reposing of the Spirit upon the Son must be distinguished from His abiding in the human nature of the incarnate Word, an abiding which is realized by the ascent from measure to measure" (Bulgakov, *The Comforter*, 249). Bulgakov distinguishes the realization as a matter of modes of relating.

36. Strauss, "Jesus and the Spirit," 266–67.

37. Dunn, *Baptism in the Holy Spirit*, 40.

assumes Jesus can partake in the benefits that stem from his act of the atonement as a whole prior to the full accomplishment of this atoning work, running contrary to the drama established by Luke's narrative (found generally throughout the Gospels), emptying the necessity of the second baptism with which Jesus must be baptized (Luke 12:50; Mark 10:38)—and the necessity of Jesus going away to receive and send his Spirit (Luke 24:49; John 7:39; 14:15–31; 16:7).[38]

Taking a different approach, N. T. Wright speaks of the Spirit's descent as looking back to the Spirit's anointing relationship "under the Old Covenant: Jesus' reception of the call to act as Israel's Messiah."[39] As the great prophets, judges, and kings are empowered by the Holy Spirit for the sake of their ministry, so is Jesus empowered by the Spirit at his baptism to *represent Israel in himself*."[40] The finalization of this work, together with its extension to the humanity represented in Jesus, is reserved for the work of the atonement as a whole, with particular emphasis on the resurrection and ascension.[41]

The key is to explain the difference between the role of the Spirit in Jesus's baptism and in his ascension, in keeping with "Luke's widely recognized tendency to emphasize the salvific importance of Jesus' exaltation over that of the crucifixion."[42] Acts 2 tells us that "God has raised this Jesus to life. . . . Exalted to the right hand of God, he has received from the Father the promised Holy Spirit and has poured out what you now see and hear" (Acts 2:32–33 NIV). What is the difference between the Spirit descending on Jesus at his baptism and Jesus's reception of the promised Holy Spirit following his ascension?

---

38. Basil seems to think of the Spirit's relation to Jesus in more continuous terms, not acknowledging the ways that the relationship takes on different modes, in keeping with the Son's incarnate role of recapitulation. Cf. Basil, *On the Holy Spirit*, 65. It seems that most interpreters follow Augustine, interpreting John 7:39 as the Spirit not yet being given to the church to the degree that it would at Pentecost, not as referring to Jesus's own experience of the Spirit. Augustine, *The Trinity*, 174. Cf. Smail, *Reflected Glory*, 107.

39. N. T. Wright, *Jesus and the Victory of God*, 536–37. Cf. Menzies, *Development of Early Christian Pneumatology*, 151; Turner, *Power from on High*, 197–201.

40. N. T. Wright, *Jesus and the Victory of God*, 537 (emphasis original).

41. Turner, *Power from on High*, 199–200.

42. Moffitt, *Rethinking the Atonement*, 243.

The difference, vital to understanding Jesus's atoning work, maps onto the Old Testament distinction between the Spirit empowering Israelites and the promise of the Spirit running throughout the Prophets. As Origen says, there is something different about "the principal coming of the Holy Spirit to human beings," which is "declared after the ascension of Christ to heaven. . . . For before that, the gift of the Holy Spirit was conferred upon only the prophets and upon a few others," but after that, "it is written that that was fulfilled *which was spoken by the prophet Joel*" (Joel 2:28).[43] Like Moses, Saul, David, and others, Jesus received the Spirit's empowering presence in his life, ordered to the fulfillment of his ministry, only to receive the great promise flowing throughout the writings of the prophets upon his resurrection and ascension.

The Spirit's relationship to the incarnate Son recapitulates the Spirit's changing relationship with different Israelites (and Israel itself), for "Israel's role is taken by her anointed king, and this Messiah has acted out her victory in himself."[44] This change (not in the eternal Son of God per se but in the "one God-human"[45]) allows for Jesus's full representation of the human condition—embracing all that it entails and transforming it from within. Prior to his own atoning work, Jesus entered "the way of penitence and obedience" at his baptism, and he was there empowered and anointed for his ministry.[46] Christ's calling was to represent not only humankind as a whole but Israel in particular, that through Israel all the families of the earth might be blessed (Gen. 12:3). His baptism marks initiation into his recapitulatory role as faithful Israel in the sight of the Father,[47] as the proper participant of the old covenant.[48] But the climax of this recapitulation comes in the role of the Spirit in the death and

43. Origen, *On First Principles*, 2:217–19 (emphasis original).
44. N. T. Wright, *The Climax of the Covenant*, 28.
45. McCormack, "'With Loud Cries and Tears,'" 55.
46. Barth, *CD* IV/1, 265. Cf. N. T. Wright, *Paul and the Faithfulness of God*, 2:258.
47. Barth, *CD* IV/1, 259.
48. Barth, *CD* IV/1, 282; cf. Turner, *Power from on High*, 199.

resurrection of Jesus, as well as the promised giving of the Spirit anticipated throughout the Old Testament.

The Spirit and Christ, Part 2: The Transforming Change

A recapitulatory reading of Christ's relation to the Spirit generates room for understanding Christ's death as the judgment of God—and therefore the Spirit—upon sinful Israel in its representative Messiah.[49] As Christ takes on human nature, he embraces the nature that is in need of saving, entering deeply and intimately into "our fallen, guilt-laden humanity, . . . our sin . . . , our violence and wickedness."[50] Jesus becomes "the one great sinner,"[51] sinlessly taking up and overcoming a reality that he himself did not will—the sinless God becoming sin in humankind's place (2 Cor. 5:21).[52] He brings humans fully into his very being in order to renew and remake them from within.[53] How does God make good on his creative purpose for humankind? And how does God do so while dealing with the problem of sin? In Jesus Christ—the one in whom we are represented, sanctified (John 17:19), and filled with the Holy Spirit.[54] It is this dynamic of representation that makes the atonement possible and that illumines the work of the Spirit in the event of Jesus's death, for Christ's bearing of sin profoundly shapes the nature of his relation to the Spirit in his atoning death.[55]

49. For an altogether different approach integrating the Spirit into the atonement in a manner eschewing this emphasis on judgment or wrath, cf. Stump, "Atonement and Eucharist," 214–16.

50. Torrance, *Mediation of Christ*, 63; cf. Johnson, *Atonement: A Guide for the Perplexed*, 46. At what point one locates Christ's sin-bearing is somewhat beside the point—even those who locate it merely on Golgotha acknowledge that at some point Jesus had to take upon himself that which he sought to heal. Our thesis merely places that point further back, either at the incarnation itself or some point prior to the passion.

51. Barth, *CD* IV/1, 251.

52. Torrance, *Atonement*, 79, 82.

53. Torrance, *Atonement*, 82.

54. Macchia likewise makes representation, bound up with a constructive account of God's love and wrath, the key to understanding the Spirit's work in the death of Jesus. Macchia, *Jesus the Spirit Baptizer*, 256–66.

55. Balthasar, *Theo-Drama*, 4:349.

It is on the cross that Christ drinks to the dregs his role as the "Judge judged in our place."[56] He is the guilty in need of judgment, such that "we are crowded out of our own place by Him in that He made our sin His own.... Made sin for us, He stands in our place."[57] But he stands in our place before the Spirit, whose role at Christ's cross was to act as the agent of his judgment in response to his being made sin, in continuity with the Old Testament model Jesus recapitulates. For as we have seen, the Spirit acts as the primary agent of divine judgment in response to disobedience and sin in the Old Testament. The Spirit departs from Saul in 1 Samuel 16:14, leaving an evil or troubling spirit in its place; in Psalm 51:11, David cries out, "Cast me not away from your presence, and take not your Holy Spirit from me." The Spirit's departure is God's "alienation from the temple," God's judgment in response to Israel's sin and wickedness, where God withdraws his saving presence, allowing chaos and death to take its place.[58]

To set this line of thought into a fully trinitarian key, some (such as Moltmann and A. Lewis) are inclined to make the Spirit the bond of love and unity between the otherwise divided Father and incarnate Son in the rupture endured on the cross.[59] But this appeal to the Spirit risks making "the Son's forsakenness on the Cross ... a directly trinitarian event,"[60] failing to incorporate the way that the incarnation of the Son—in particular, his sin-bearing—changes the

56. Barth, *CD* IV/1, 204.
57. Barth, *CD* IV/1, 234.
58. Block, *Book of Ezekiel*, 1:326.
59. A. Lewis, *Between Cross and Resurrection*, 251–52; Wynne, *Wrath among the Perfections of God's Life*, 172; Cole, *God the Peacemaker*, 166–67; Moltmann, *Crucified God*. Barth goes so far as to speak of the Spirit "maintaining [God's] unity as Father and Son, God in the love which unites Him as Father with the Son, and Son with the Father" (*CD* IV/1, 308), but he does so without positing a tension or disunity between Father and Son to be overcome by the Spirit. The key is to see the Spirit not as uniting the Father and Son but as the unity of the Father and Son: "From the fact that the Father and the Son mutually love one another, it necessarily follows that this mutual Love, the Holy Ghost, proceeds from them both." Thomas Aquinas, *ST* I.37.1.
60. Balthasar, *Theo-Drama*, 4:322.

mode of relating between Father, incarnate Son, and Holy Spirit. It
is likewise unworthy of the way the triune God actively and unit-
edly wills the cross of Jesus, as well as the way God extends his self,
his love, to his sinful creation, his sinful people. God's mission is to
extend or repeat in time God's life with that of the creature.[61] God's
love, when extended or repeated in time and therefore directed (at
least in part) toward sin, takes the form, the mode, of wrath, abandonment, and judgment. The Spirit, who is God and therefore love
(1 John 4:8), *is* the wrath of the Father and the Son when directed
against sin, for God's nature is "indivisible, and [his] activity is one.
The Father does all things through the Word in the Holy Spirit,"[62] a
claim that is just as true of God's love in the mode of wrath as it is of
God's love per se, for God's wrath *is* God's love, in an oppositional
mode.[63] To Maximos's claim that "the Father was present by approving the incarnation, while the Holy Spirit *cooperated* with the Son
who carried it out," we can and should add that in the cross, the
Father pours out wrath upon sin through the sin-bearing, incarnate

61. This is my generalization of Vidu's helpful point that "since a mission extends a procession to include a created effect, the mission of the Spirit, extending as it does the procession of
the Spirit, repeats in time the procession of the Spirit from the Father and the Son (*filioque*)"
(Vidu, "Ascension and Pentecost," 103). Vidu is concerned that "some authors have suggested
that the reason Christ cannot send the Spirit prior to his ascension is because he has yet to
receive the Spirit as a reward," and this entails that "the Spirit must be seen as extrinsic to
Christ, something that he receives from the outside" (103–4). Our position integrates both
Vidu's commitment to Chalcedonian Christology and his idea that the mission of the Spirit
is to repeat in time the eternal procession of the Spirit with the implications of Christ being
the sin bearer, such that this repetition in time involves a changing relationship between the
Spirit and the humanity of the eternal Son. The change is not between the Spirit and the
Son but between the Spirit and the sin-bearing Jesus, who is recapitulating the relationship
of Israel and the Holy Spirit for us and for our salvation. The changing presence of the Spirit
is put "not in terms of a change in God, but rather as a change in the creature's relation to
God"—namely, the creature Jesus, the representative of Israel ("Ascension and Pentecost,"
106). Vidu's concern that this implies that "God enables himself to do this or that through
some created action" is off the mark in this case, for it is rather God enabling Jesus to do
this or that. The change is in Jesus, as creature, rather than a change in God himself (109).

62. Athanasius, *Letters concerning the Holy Spirit*, 135.

63. "A dogmatic account of God's wrath is largely determined by that particular intercession wherein God sacrificially takes upon himself the destructive power of his own oppositional work." Wynne, *Wrath among the Perfections of God's Life*, 169.

Word, by the work of the Holy Spirit, and in this way, the triune God loves and therefore judges sinful humankind in Jesus.[64] The Spirit is thus the unity and love of the Father and the Son, as shaped by the latter being the incarnate sin bearer;[65] as such, the Spirit is the wrath of God against sin. "The Son bears sinners within himself, together with the hopeless impenetrability of their sin, which prevents the divine light of love from registering in them. In himself, therefore, he experiences . . . the hopelessness of their resistance to God and the graceless No of divine grace to this resistance"[66]—the "No" that is the wrath of the Father, directed toward sin in the sin-bearing Son, in the power of the Holy Spirit. The unity of God is just as true in the act of opposing sin in the sin bearer as it is in the eternal life of God as Father, Son, and Holy Spirit.

What was the role of the Spirit in the atonement? To be the love of God directed toward the sin bearer; to be the love of God in its mode of wrath. Such a view does not posit, with Moltmann, any sort of rupture within the Trinity. Rather, it reaffirms the Trinity in unity precisely at the point of the cross, exercising God's self against sin for our sake and for our salvation. The view does so by acknowledging the love and therefore the wrath of God against sin—not toward us and our destruction but taking these up within the life of the triune God via the sin-bearing of Jesus, that through the united work of Father, incarnate Son, and Holy Spirit, God might make the problem of sin his own, dealing with our problem on the basis of the resources proper and unique to the divine, triune life.[67]

Jesus, the Old Testament man commissioned for ministry at his baptism by the descent of the Holy Spirit, continues under this Old Testament paradigm through his death, and he is judged as the representative of Israel by the Father through the Holy Spirit at the

---

64. Maximos, *Expositio orationis dominicae* (CCSG 23:31–32, lines 87–89), cited in Blowers, *Maximus the Confessor*, 147 (emphasis added).

65. Balthasar, *Theo-Drama*, 4:346. Balthasar is interacting with Barth, *CD* II/1, 396.

66. Balthasar, *Theo-Drama*, 4:349.

67. Johnson, *Atonement: A Guide for the Perplexed*, 59–87.

cross. Only in this judgment, only in experiencing the Spirit's nour-ishing and empowering presence in its mode of judgment upon sin, is Christ's consistent representation of sinful Israel preserved. Only through the Spirit's judgment can Christ "deliv[er] up sinful man and sin in His own person."[68]

Resurrection, Ascension, and the Gift of the Spirit

But delivering up sinful humanity is not the goal of the Messiah—far from it! Peter tells us that "this Jesus God raised up, and of that we all are witnesses. Being therefore exalted at the right hand of God, and having received from the Father the promise of the Holy Spirit, he has poured out this that you yourselves are seeing and hearing" at Pentecost (Acts 2:32–33). And Calvin writes that "Christ indeed does not cleanse us by his blood, nor render God propitious to us by his expiation, in any other way than by making us partakers of his Spirit, who renews us to a holy life."[69] The question is this: What is this promise that Jesus received, and how does it bear upon our understanding of the Spirit's role in the atonement? As Moffitt puts it,

> The narrative of Acts suggests that the experience of the gift of the Spirit's outpouring led Jesus's early followers to assume that he had done something to make them pure in some new and amazing way, and their logic worked the same way with respect to Cornelius. If this is right, then the inference seems to follow that Jesus actually made some kind of sacrifice that purified people *to the point that they could be recipients of God's own Holy Spirit.*[70]

The atonement is not merely a matter of overcoming evil, but first and foremost of establishing goodness (in part through overcoming

68. Barth, *CD* IV/1, 246.
69. Calvin, *Commentaries on Romans*, 219.
70. Moffitt, *Rethinking the Atonement*, 254 (emphasis added).

evil): "an act of perfecting grace, completing what was begun when the Spirit, who long ago brooded over the waters and brought forth life on earth, hovered over Mary, . . . [which] fully establishes the communion between God and man at which God was already aiming in creation itself."[71] And while the former may be entailed in the latter, the order is vital. God became human not simply to die, not merely to judge sin, but to bring God's creative project to completion in the Messiah of Israel, through him blessing every family of the earth (Gen. 12:3). While the judgment of the Spirit is therefore a vital part of Christ's work, this is but a preliminary step toward a higher purpose, a part though not the whole of his recapitulatory work—for "Jesus's death was an essential *part* of the larger process of his atoning sacrifice."[72] For the true goal of the Messiah, in whom the history of Israel and therefore creation itself was to be completed, lay in the prophesied Holy Spirit, who would render "mortal humanity fit to draw near to God's presence."[73] As Edwards puts it, "The Father provides the Saviour or purchaser, and the purchase is made of him; and the Son is the purchaser and the price; and the Holy Spirit is the great blessing or inheritance purchased, as is intimated, Gal. iii. 13, 14; and hence the Spirit is often spoken of as the sum of the blessings promised in the gospel."[74] In short, Christ became a curse for us so that in Christ Jesus we might receive the blessing of the promised Spirit (Gal. 3:13–14)—a summary of the gospel we are now able to appreciate pneumatologically, for Christ's work of becoming a curse and suffering judgment was just as much a work of the Spirit as was

71. Farrow, *Ascension Theology*, 122.

72. Moffitt, *Rethinking the Atonement*, 258 (emphasis original).

73. Moffitt, *Rethinking the Atonement*, 248.

74. Edwards, *Religious Affections*, 162. S. Holmes writes, "I am happy to accept this as a theological claim, but it once again seems to be a move beyond the logic of penal substitution; it is not a claim that can be made sense of within the logic of the law court. If we believe that penal substitution is an exhaustive account of what happens at the atonement, then, the claim of a Trinitarian, specifically pneumatological, deficit is plausible" ("Penal Substitution," 300). Our argument is that Jesus experienced the judgment of the Spirit so that he might be freed from our sin, which he was bearing. This binds the Spirit to penal substitution, without necessarily making the latter an exhaustive account of the cross.

Christ's reception and sharing of the Spirit upon his resurrection and ascension.

Jesus's first baptism (by John) was necessary, but its true goal was his second baptism, the baptism of his death and resurrection, in which we participate through our own baptism (Rom. 6:1–14). The judgment of the sin bearer was necessary that he might be sanctified,[75] "sanctifying our humanity entirely in his own person";[76] that he might be cleansed of the sin he was bearing (for Jesus, too, the Spirit is the "Spirit of sanctification"[77]); that after his resurrection and ascension, he might prove to be a fit temple for the full blessing of the Holy Spirit and, as such, might share the Spirit with those built up in him as a part of his temple, as a part of his body.[78] "Only when a man has been cleansed from the shame of his evil, and has returned to his natural beauty, and the original form of the Royal Image has been restored in him, is it possible for him to approach the Paraclete"—a claim as true of the sin bearer as those represented and recapitulated in him.[79]

Why did God become human? That as human he might be made fit for and receive the promised Holy Spirit, sharing it with those united to and represented in him, bringing creation to its Spirit-saturated end, to its goal as the city of God, where men and women "live according to the spirit" of Jesus Christ.[80] "Henceforth the Holy Spirit reposes upon the God-man" and those united to him by faith, "just as He eternally reposes on the Logos."[81] God became man that *as human* he might partake of the Holy Spirit as fully as he does *as the divine Son*—that he might share the Spirit with those who have been justified and sanctified in him.

---

75. Cyril of Alexandria, *On the Unity of Christ*, 100. Cf. Torrance, *Theology in Recon-struction*, 248.

76. Farrow, *Ascension Theology*, 123.

77. Athanasius, *Letters concerning the Holy Spirit*, 87. Cf. Thomas Aquinas, *ST* I.42.7.

78. Cf. Scully, *Physicalist Soteriology in Hilary of Poitiers*, 218–19; Leithart, *Delivered from the Elements of the World*, 169–74.

79. Basil, *On the Holy Spirit*, 44.

80. Augustine, *City of God* 14.1, p. 581. Cf. Tanner, *Christ the Key*, 170–71.

81. Bulgakov, *The Comforter*, 256. Cf. McCormack, "'With Loud Cries and Tears,'" 55.

Conclusion

It is when the life of Christ is seen to mirror and fulfill Israel's relationship with the Holy Spirit that we find a consistent understanding of
the Spirit's role in Christ's atoning death, resurrection, and ascension.
The Spirit's resting upon Jesus sets the stage for future movement
within the Spirit's relationship with Jesus, anticipating the judgment
of Jesus as the sin-bearing recapitulation of Israel by the Spirit at the
event of his death. The Spirit proves to function as the main agent
of Christ's judgment, akin to the Spirit's role in Israel and the temple
in the Old Testament, as the mode of God's love in the presence of
sin—wrath. The fulfillment of the Spirit's work, however, lies in the
further work of the Spirit in Jesus, sanctifying and filling the incarnate Son in the full sense anticipated in Old Testament prophecy,
that Jesus might share the Spirit with all those united in him.[82] The
atonement, we conclude, is a work not merely of the Father and the
Son, the benefits of which are applied by the Spirit; the atonement is
the one work of the one God: Father, incarnate Son, and Holy Spirit.

But is this too much of a stretch? Is there too little to go on in
Scripture and in the history of theology to allow for such bold claims?
Could we preach such a view of the role of the Holy Spirit within
the doctrine of the atonement? Essentially, this boils down to the
following questions: Must worship of the triune God be safe, confident, and secure? Or does it also have the freedom, the liberty, to be
joyful, playful, and creative? God wants to be known; he wants to be
worshiped for who he is and what he has done for us. And what of
those areas where something must be said, where something must be
true, but we are not exactly sure of what to say? Where we have good
reason to believe something but nothing close to certainty? Where
we would gladly be wrong, gladly learn from others—and yet, for

---

82. Though we do not develop the point here, one implication of this essay is that it offers
an important avenue for dialogue between Pentecostal branches of the church, with their
insight into the person and work of the Holy Spirit, and those branches of the church that
tend to emphasize the person and work of the Son. Cf. Smail, *Reflected Glory*, 104.

the time being, what we do say is the best we have to offer, the best
our understanding can do, as an act of faithfulness? This, I believe, is
where theology is at its best. Humble, thankful, joyful, exploratory—
a boldly tentative exploration of faith seeking understanding, or of
worship in its most playful and creative mode.

DOXOLOGICAL INTERLUDE

Thomas Traherne's Centuries of Meditations

Yet you must arm yourself with expectations of their [others'] infirmi-
ties, and resolve nobly to forgive them: not in a sordid and cowardly
manner, by taking no notice of them, nor in a dim and lazy manner,
by letting them alone: but in a divine and illustrious manner by chiding
them meekly, and vigorously rendering and showering down all kind of
benefits. Cheerfully continuing to do good, and whatever you suffer
by your piety and charity, confidence or love, to be like our Saviour,
unwearied: who when He was abused and had often been evil-intreated
among men, proceeded courageously through all treacheries and deceits
to die for them. So shall you turn their very vices, into virtues, to you,
and, as our Saviour did, make of a wreath of thorns a crown of glory.
But set the splendour of virtues before you, and when some fail, think
with yourself, there are some sincere and excellent, and why should not
I be the most virtuous?[1]

---

1. Thomas Traherne, *Centuries of Meditations* 1.84 (p. 61).

CHAPTER FIVE

Atonement and the Christian Life

WHAT IS THE ROLE of Christ's atonement in the Christian life? How are we to be shaped in word, deed, and soul by Jesus's death and resurrection, or how, to tap into one of the major themes of this book, does the doctrine of the atonement shape our worship? The problem is not so much what we can say but where to begin, for we cannot possibly do the topic justice in a chapter or even a book, for that matter. We are to have in ourselves the mind of Christ (Phil. 2:5)—the mindset rooted in the character of God that governed his death and resurrection. But as the church, my own small church included, continually falls far short of this calling, it is simultaneously a matter of doctrine, of reflecting on the calling and identity we have in the risen Lord Jesus, which we will live up to only in glory. To organize our reflection on this theme, we will dwell on the doctrine of the church, for the atonement is a matter of the Christian life only because it pertains to the church, within which Christians live out their lives in and before their Lord.

Genesis tells us that God said, "'Let us make man in our image, after our likeness. And let them have dominion over the fish of the sea and over the birds of the heavens and over the livestock and over all the earth and over every creeping thing that creeps on the earth.' So God created man in his own image, / in the image of God he created him; / male and female he created them. And God blessed them" (Gen. 1:26–28). What does it mean to be made in God's image? We could attend to the differences between humans and the beasts over which they are to rule (1:28) or to the role of "image" in ancient Near Eastern contexts, but Paul takes us in a rather different direction. The mystery of marriage, he says, is "profound . . . and refers to Christ and the church" (Eph. 5:32). Adam and Eve, together with the marriage they portray, were made in the image of God as a preparation for—a tangible portrayal of—a deeper, underlying mystery: that of the union of Christ and his bride. For Christ "loved the church and gave himself up for her, that he might sanctify her, having cleansed her by the washing of water with the word, so that he might present the church to himself in splendor, without spot or wrinkle or any such thing, that she might be holy and without blemish" (Eph. 5:25–27).

What, according to Paul, does it mean to be made in the image of God? It means not simply to be human, not simply to have some quality, characteristic, or feature, but to be redeemed, sanctified, and cleansed, united to Christ, that through this union of husband and wife, of Christ and his church, we might image forth the life and character of God in his creation.[1] In Ephesians, Paul explores this imaging in terms of holiness: Christ's work is to cleanse us from our uncleanness that we might be holy as God is holy, reflecting and portraying the holiness of God and thereby fulfilling the great call of Israel (Lev. 11:44). In fulfillment of the Pentateuch and the creation of humankind and the calling of Israel, in completion of the prophetic critique and longing, the holy God becomes man that he might take upon himself our uncleanness, bearing it that we in turn might be cleansed, sanctified—might participate in his cleanness, his holiness.

1. R. S. Peterson, *The* Imago Dei *as Human Identity*.

And this story, of course, can be told over and over again, in light of not merely God's holiness but his righteousness, love, patience, goodness, wisdom, steadfastness, and so forth. God took up our likeness that we might be remade in his. For that is the logic of this marriage. According to Luther,

> By this solemn vow, as the Apostle Paul teaches, Christ and the soul become one flesh. And if they are one flesh, there is a true marriage between them—indeed, the most perfect of marriages, because human marriages are but a shadow of this one true union. Given the marriage between Christ and the soul, it follows that they hold everything in common, the good as well as the evil. Accordingly, the soul that trusts Christ can boast and glory in him since it regards what he has as its own. And it follows that whatever the soul has Christ claims as his own.
>
> Let us look at this exchange in more detail and we shall be able to see its invaluable benefits. Christ is full of grace, life, and salvation while the soul is full of sins, death, and damnation. Now let faith enter the picture and sins, death, and damnation are Christ's while grace, life, and salvation will be the soul's. For if Christ is a bridegroom he must take upon himself that which are his bride's, and he in turn bestows on her all that is his. If he gives her his body and very self, how shall he not give her all that is his? And if he takes the body of his bride, how shall he not take all that is hers?[2]

Christ bestows on us all that is his—but what is his? Paul tells us,

> He is the image of the invisible God, the firstborn of all creation. For by him all things were created, in heaven and on earth, visible and invisible, whether thrones or dominions or rulers or authorities—all things were created through him and for him. And he is before all things, and in him all things hold together. And he is the head of the body, the church. He is the beginning, the firstborn from the dead, that in everything he might be preeminent. For in him all the fullness

2. Luther, *Freedom of a Christian*, 409–10.

of God was pleased to dwell, and through him to reconcile to himself
all things, whether on earth or in heaven, making peace by the blood
of his cross. (Col. 1:15–20)

What is his? Everything—for by him all things were made, and all
things are for him. All things hold together in him. He is preeminent.
The whole fullness of God dwells in him, and all things are reconciled
to him. What is Christ's? The whole of creation, and the fullness of
God. His by creation, and his by redemption. This he bestows on us.

What, then, is the relationship between the atonement and the
Christian life? To live into our marriage with Jesus Christ and what
we are and have in him. We are not yet glorified, presented to Christ,
shining and spotless. The Lord has not yet returned in glory. But the
calling is the same: to live into the reality of our life in Christ, the
church's union with the bridegroom.

In what follows, we will explore one aspect of the church living
into this reality: forgiveness. For as Barth says, "The way of the Christian is derived from the forgiveness of sins."[3] And as Webster makes
clear, "The practice of Christian theology will involve the cultivation
of persons with specific habits of mind and soul"[4]—and one of the
central practices among these is that of forgiveness. For if our goal
is indeed worship, then before we worship, we must forgive those
against whom we have something to forgive (Mark 11:25–26).

The Inner Basis of Forgiveness: Reconciliation

One of the key marks of the church of Jesus Christ is that it is one.
Think, for instance, of Jesus's prayer:

I do not ask for these only, but also for those who will believe in me
through their word, that they may all be one, just as you, Father, are
in me, and I in you, that they also may be in us, so that the world

3. Barth, *Dogmatics in Outline*, 149.
4. Webster, *Culture of Theology*, 45.

may believe that you have sent me. The glory that you have given me I have given to them, that they may be one even as we are one, I in them and you in me, that they may become perfectly one, so that the world may know that you sent me and loved them even as you loved me. (John 17:20–23)

The strife and division attending the first marriage ("Your desire will be for your husband, and he will rule over you" [Gen. 3:16 NIV]), the first family (Cain's murder of Abel and response to the Lord: "Am I my brother's keeper?" [Gen. 4:9]), the first peoples (Gen. 6), and Jew and gentile are all encapsulated in the dereliction of Jesus, his cry from the cross, and his death, his return to the earth from which Adam was made. The bridegroom takes our isolation, our abandonment, our strife, that we in turn might have something that seems almost blasphemous to say: that we might be one—not as a husband and wife are one, not as two dear friends or a mother and daughter are one, but as the triune God, Father, Son, and Holy Spirit, is one. "Hear, O Israel: The LORD our God, the LORD is one" (Deut. 6:4). Even as God is one, even as Father and Son are one—that is Christ's prayer for us, the purpose of his work of at-one-ment.

This oneness demands a holistic approach to the church's ministry of reconciliation. Paul writes that God

> through Christ reconciled us to himself and gave us the ministry of reconciliation; that is, in Christ God was reconciling the world to himself, not counting their trespasses against them [forgiveness], and entrusting to us the message of reconciliation. Therefore, we are ambassadors for Christ, God making his appeal through us.... For our sake he made him to be sin who knew no sin, so that in him we might become the righteousness of God [atonement]. (2 Cor. 5:18–21)

At the very root of the Christian life, therefore, stands a ministry, a vocation, that integrates forgiveness and atonement. God has not only reconciled us to himself but given us a ministry. And that ministry involves a message, an appeal, that comes from the specific content of the gospel: "For our sake he made him to be sin who knew no sin, so that in him we might become the righteousness of God." Those who are a new creation in Christ (2 Cor. 5:17) are to put on the mind of Christ (1 Cor. 2:16) and, therefore, to long for unity, oneness, and reconciliation. Negatively, we are to regard no one according to the flesh (2 Cor. 5:16). Positively, we are to be shaped by the content of the message we proclaim, inviting others into the unity God seeks to share with us—a unity of godly righteousness. And this is our worship—the obedient, receptive union of understanding and action in response to the work and command of our Savior.

Forgiveness

At root, this calling entails something extraordinarily difficult that goes right to the heart of the gospel. As Calvin puts it, "Forgiveness of sins, then, is for us the first entry into the church and Kingdom of God. Without it, there is for us no covenant or bond with God."[5] For our sakes, God "made [Jesus] to be sin who knew no sin," and he did not count the world's "trespasses against them" (2 Cor. 5:19–21). And we, like Christ, are called, commanded even, to forgive. "And whenever you stand praying, forgive, if you have anything against anyone, so that your Father also who is in heaven may forgive you your trespasses" (Mark 11:25). To be clear, forgiveness is not the whole work of the church—"it should not be approached in an atomized way, but rather as part of a wide process of reconciliation and peace building"[6]—but it is a vital work nonetheless.

Forgiveness is precisely where much of liberal theology in the nineteenth century began—with a gospel of forgiveness, but one over and against traditional understandings of the doctrine of the

5. Calvin, *Institutes* IV.i.21 (p. 1034).

6. Smyth, "Brokenness, Forgiveness, Healing, and Peace in Ireland," 322. Much harm comes, it seems, from trying to load too much into one's understanding of forgiveness, such that it becomes indistinguishable, for instance, from reconciliation or justice.

atonement.[7] Writing of Jesus's reconciling work, Adolf von Harnack asks, "Christ died for our sins? Christ has reconciled God? How? Did God require a reconciliation? Is God not Love? Does the God who forgives sins, the God of mercy, require an indemnity? Did the Father in the parable of the lost son demand expiation before he forgave his son?"[8] Harnack's answer is that "God is Love. . . . The consolation of the Gospel of Jesus consists, indeed, in this—that He has revealed unto us God as eternal love. Far be the thought from us that God has been turned from wrath to love, and that something had to be paid or sacrificed in order that He might love and forgive."[9] Harnack then describes the punishment inflicted on sin as stemming from a "conception of God" as "a wrathful judge"—a conception that is the necessary consequence of our sin and godlessness. Wrath is not an attribute of God, a description of his stance toward sin; it is, rather, a phantasm generated by a tormented conscience—a psychological state of self-inflicted punishment. Jesus's work is that of "convincing sinners that forgiving Love is mightier than the Justice before which they tremble."[10] The dichotomy is clear: in our sin, we conceive of God as a wrathful judge—and this is its own form of punishment— but Jesus reveals to us an altogether different God, a forgiving God of love, particularly in what Harnack considers the great summary of the gospel, the parable of the prodigal son.

Our challenge is to integrate these concepts into a picture of a just *and* loving God, a God of atonement *and* forgiveness. As Murray puts it so clearly:

> This espousal of forgiveness and the atonement within the life of God is only achieved by a theological perspective that affirms the reality of the wrath of God. This is because reconciliation is not mere inclusion

---

7. Cf. Collett, "Book of the Twelve," 411–14. In many ways, the roots of this liberal "gospel of forgiveness" lie in Socinus's critique. Cf. van den Brink, "Hugo Grotius."

8. Harnack, "Atonement," 17.

9. Harnack, "Atonement," 18.

10. Harnack, "Atonement," 19.

of the enemy, nor is justification mere acceptance of injustice.... Evil that is accomplished must be condemned and overcome.... Divine wrath is God's stance of active opposition to evil, and to think other- wise would be to depict God as "an indifferent demon who would condemn men and women to indifference."[11]

And as Barth puts it, "If God does not meet us in His jealous zeal and wrath ... then He does not meet us at all, and in spite of all our asseverations about divine love, man is in actual fact left to himself. That man is not abandoned in this way, that God is really gracious to him, is shown in the fact that God confronts him in holiness."[12]

What Forgiveness Is Not

To counteract a view of forgiveness rooted in the dichotomy between love and justice, we begin with what forgiveness is not, for the danger of misunderstanding is significant: forgiveness is not a simple con- cept.[13] Forgiveness is certainly *not* a matter of passing over evil, look- ing the other way, pretending evil did not happen, forgetting that it happened, ignoring its consequences for both perpetrator and victim, or merely overcoming negative feelings or reactions to the wrong.[14] For my wife to forgive me is not for her to understand things from my perspective, to pretend that my hurtful action did not happen,

11. Murray, *Reclaiming Divine Wrath*, 245. Murray is here citing Volf, "Divine Violence," 972.

12. Barth, *CD* II/1, 366.

13. Habets, "'To Err Is Human, to Forgive Is Divine,'" 4. Cf. Barth, *CD* IV/2, 772: "God's love is total grace for sinful man, but also total judgment over him. It is total grace because it is God's perfect turning and goodness and friendliness. ... But it is also total judgment because it is the holy severity of God."

14. According to Warmke, Nelkin, and McKenna, accounts of forgiveness typically focus on one's emotions, on forbearance of revenge or punishment, or on certain kinds of perfor- mance ("Forgiveness," 8–15). This chapter allows for these, but it provides a theological ac- count of forgiveness that is distinct from all of them. "The concept of Christian forgiveness ... is not merely an anthropological understanding of what forgiveness effects. The mercy God introduces to the world in Christ and asks believers to share is wholly new." Coutts, *A Shared Mercy*, 95.

that she was not hurt, that I did not wrong her; nor is it simply to overcome her anger. We reject any account that minimizes, enables, or leaves evil to its own devices, any view that makes forgiveness merely a matter of the internal state of the forgiver or merely a matter of the punishment of or consequences for the forgiven.

Anselm asks "whether it is fitting for God to forgive a sin out of mercy alone, without any restitution of what is owed to him."[15] His answer is that forgiveness, understood this way, leaves sin un-regulated by law, leaving it in a position of great freedom, effectively making sin and holiness equal.[16] But the equality, of course, is merely ephemeral—and quite different than it seems. On the surface, this leaves the perpetrator in the position of power, with the lawful and innocent hampered by law (the "shackles" of the law under which Commissioner Gordon works in Christopher Nolan's Batman trilogy comes to mind). But at a deeper level, things are even worse than this. Forgiveness in the sense of merely ignoring sin, as though it hadn't happened, abandons the perpetrator to the internal and external dynamics of their sin; it abandons them, as Milton would put it, to the hell they carry with them.[17] The victim is left to suffer their pain; the perpetrator is left to suffer hell.

What Forgiveness Is: A Preliminary Overview

Forgiveness is not first and foremost about our feelings, our sense of wrong, our desire to be free from painful memories; it is not primarily psychological, sociological, or political. It is all these things, of course, but they are not the heart, the defining aspect, of forgiveness. The biblical understanding of forgiveness is something we do *in relation to God*, as we have been forgiven by him.[18] It is something

15. Anselm, *Why God Became Man* 1.12 (pp. 284–86).
16. As Coutts puts it, "Forgiveness without judgment simply decides that sin is *good*, or at least *understandable*." Coutts, *A Shared Mercy*, 138 (emphasis original).
17. Milton, *Paradise Lost*, 4.20–26.
18. Cf. Coutts, *A Shared Mercy*, 115.

that enters the anthropological sphere only because of the work of
God among us. "Only by returning to the ontological foundations
of forgiveness found in the external works of God, especially in the
Incarnation, can a proper basis be found for then conducting in-
terpersonal forgiveness."[19] Forgiveness, in other words, is a properly
theological reality, and only for that reason does it enter and play
itself out in the different dimensions of our lives. And it is a reality
that "presupposes that justice—full justice in the strict sense of the
term"—has been done in Christ's death and resurrection.[20]

In the book of Genesis, after a prolonged test of his brothers (forgiveness is perfectly compatible with the use of wisdom to test and
understand), Joseph forgives them, refusing to pay them back, asking,
"Am I in the place of God? As for you, you meant evil against me, but
God meant it for good" (Gen. 50:19–20). Forgiveness is something
Joseph is free to do, and it is something we can likewise do because
we find ourselves in the larger context of the work and story of God;
it is an act we are freed to do as we operate and are sustained by the
larger kingdom of God.[21] "What forgiveness does is entrust these
things entirely to God and proceed in the freedom of faith. . . . The
residual effects of past sin are still there to be dealt with, but are re-
oriented to the accomplished reconciliation and provisional healing
of Christ."[22] God, as revealed in Scripture, is a forgiving God. "The
LORD, the LORD, a God merciful and gracious, slow to anger, and

19. Habets, "'To Err Is Human, to Forgive Is Divine,'" 3. Cf. Petersen, "Theology of
Forgiveness," 11. Lippitt makes a similar point (though he has in mind something rather
more immanent and less theological in his interaction with Blustein's *Forgiveness and Re-
membrance*), speaking of "assimilat[ing] such emotional reactions to wrongdoing into 'new
structures' of belief and expectation, such that these intrusive memories 'are rendered less
salient.'" Lippitt, *Love's Forgiveness*, 150.

20. Volf, "Forgiveness, Reconciliation, and Justice," 46. Dawson's claim (many others make
similar claims) that "at the cross mercy triumphed over justice," that forgiveness is opposed
to full justice, ultimately entails the claim that justice is foreign to the character of God and,
therefore, the fundamental pattern of human life—a conclusion Scripture forbids us to make.
Dawson, "Hatred's End," 219.

21. On forgiveness as an act, cf. J. C. Rutledge, *Forgiveness and Atonement*, 67.

22. Coutts, *A Shared Mercy*, 117.

abounding in steadfast love and faithfulness, keeping steadfast love
for thousands, forgiving iniquity and transgression and sin, but who
will by no means clear the guilty" (Exod. 34:6–7; cf. Num. 14:19).
God is a God of forgiveness. He is not a slave to it, not forced to forgive, and he is one who at times revokes forgiveness (Matt. 18:21–35)
and does not forgive (Deut. 29:20; Josh. 24:19)—but he is a God
of forgiveness, nonetheless. But Exodus 34:6–7 and Numbers 14:19
do more than establish God as a forgiving God; they set up a tension
that frames our understanding of forgiveness. God forgives iniquity
and transgression, but he will by no means clear the guilty. But aren't
the guilty precisely the ones he forgives? Forgiveness, it turns out,
is more than simply a matter of not holding someone's sin against
them. It is a matter of dealing appropriately with that sin and, *in this
way*, not holding their sin against them.

Hebrews 9:22 affirms that "under the law almost everything is
purified with blood, and without the shedding of blood there is no
forgiveness of sins." There are prerequisites for forgiveness, and there
are conditions for maintaining it. God's love is unconditional in the
sense that we do not earn or cause it, but that does not mean that
forgiveness is entirely without conditions, dynamics, or boundaries.[23] In fact, the opposite is true. Love and the forgiveness it enacts
have conditions, in the sense that they have their own proper order,
logic, and components. Forgiveness and the love that stands behind
it are not arbitrary, random, or illogical;[24] they have their reasons,
patterns, preconditions, and purposes.[25] Paul, in the Letter to the

23. Rigby, "Forgiveness," 494–95. Cf. Swinburne, "Forgiving as a Performative Utterance,"
141; Coutts, *A Shared Mercy*, 122. Stump, on the other hand, develops an account of love and
forgiveness that is utterly unilateral, rejecting anything to do with what she calls "Anselmian"
views of the atonement, in which some preconditions exist in God, rooted in his justice and
holiness, for instance, for extending love to sinners (Stump, *Atonement*, 71–112). "God's
forgiveness," she writes, "like God's love, is unilateral and unconditional. It does not depend
on anything; rather it is a function of God's nature, which is perfectly good and therefore
also perfectly loving" (101).

24. This is Wolterstorff's fear as summed up in Lippitt, *Love's Forgiveness*, 117.

25. I mean something rather different from Lippitt's two kinds of "conditional forgiveness," both of which have to do with preconditions that must be met in the wrongdoer

Colossians, develops this line of thought: we, "who were dead in [our] trespasses . . . , God made alive together with [Christ], having forgiven us all our trespasses, by canceling the record of debt that stood against us with its legal demands. This he set aside, nailing it to the cross" (Col. 2:13–14). There is a means by which forgiveness is accomplished. And this opens up a corresponding ethic for the church: "Bear with each other and forgive one another if any of you has a grievance against someone. Forgive as the Lord forgave you" (3:13 NIV). Forgiveness, at the very least, entails real sin and trespass and a motion or movement accomplished by means of a proper activity, a twofold work: "by canceling the record of debt," by "nailing it to the cross." More must be said, but forgiveness is here accomplished, brought about, not merely by a movement of the will or a change in emotions but by an efficient action, a form of dealing with the underlying problem of sin.

The point is that *forgiveness, while it is freely proclaimed, is not in fact freely given.*[26] As Fleming Rutledge reiterates throughout her book *The Crucifixion*, "Forgiveness is not enough!" By that she means the cheap forgiveness of liberal theology rooted in the fatherly mercy of God (in opposition to other aspects of God's character and will revealed in Scripture)—not the costly and holistic forgiveness effected by the passion of Jesus (Heb. 9:21–28), the "destroying of sin which takes place in the death of Christ, the purging of it accomplished in the blood of Christ."[27] Forgiveness, according to Scripture, is a complex work. It involves conditions both in its beginning and in the dynamic or pattern it creates. Forces are at play, characters are in action, purposes are accomplished; the whole gospel story—the recapitulation of the Old Testament in the work of the Messiah—

---

before the victim can or should forgive. Conditional forgiveness as I mean it pertains to the conditions God must bring about in order to be faithful to himself in forgiving, as well as to the way this serves as the precondition for our own forgiveness of others. Lippitt, *Love's Forgiveness*, 62.

26. Cf. F. Rutledge, *The Crucifixion*, 126, 141–43, 325–30, 594–96, 610–11.
27. Barth, *CD* IV/1, 256. Bonhoeffer's "costly grace" comes to mind.

culminates, we might say, in the forgiveness of sins brought about by the death and resurrection of Jesus. God forgave us *by* the cross, and on that basis, he commands that those forgiven by him extend forgiveness to others. Jesus's blood was poured out *for* the forgiveness of sins. Forgiveness, according to Scripture, was accomplished by a certain means,[28] a necessary and costly way of making it happen, and that same "complexity of process"[29] continues to shape the life and action of those who are forgiven.[30] Jesus's sacrificial death accomplished, was the effective way of bringing about, forgiveness of sin, and the forgiven are commanded to imitate, to participate in, his life.

But why and how is it the case that Jesus's passion brought about the forgiveness of sins? Why didn't God simply say "Your sins are forgiven" and leave it at that? Partly, it is for negative reasons. As we have mentioned already, an account of forgiveness such as this (in which God simply forgives sin) leaves sinners in their sin. Such forgiveness is not a blessing but a curse. As Anselm puts it, such an account leaves sin unregulated, makes sinning and not sinning equivalent, leaves sin subject to no law.[31] To forgive in this way is to leave the sinner in their sin, with all its internal and relational dynamics and consequences. Without question, we owe our great sympathy to victims for the

28. As Petersen puts it (summarizing Bonhoeffer), forgiveness entails a cost and a medium—a way or movement in order to bring something about ("Theology of Forgiveness," 19). See Calvin's similar point: "But the best passage of all on this matter is the one in which [Paul] teaches that the sum of the gospel embassy is to reconcile us to God, since God is willing to receive us into grace through Christ, not counting our sins against us [II Cor. 5:18–20]. Let my readers carefully ponder the whole passage. For a little later Paul adds by way of explanation: 'Christ, who was without sin, was made sin for us' [II Cor. 5:21], to designate the means of reconciliation [cf. vs. 18–19]" (Calvin, *Institutes* III.xi.4 [p. 729]). Cf. McKenny, "Freedom, Responsibility, and Moral Agency," 315–16.

29. Smyth, "Brokenness, Forgiveness, Healing, and Peace in Ireland," 334.

30. The negative definition of *forgiveness*, rooted in the concept of not holding, not counting, or not reckoning, leads J. C. Rutledge to an elaboration of forgiveness without a means for dealing with sin, so far as I can tell, such that the forgiver resorts to what I think of as moral fiction: treating "a wrongdoer as if they are *excusable*" or "as if he is not morally blameworthy" (Rutledge, *Forgiveness and Atonement*, 79–80). While rooted in Scripture, this account falls short of a comprehensive picture by largely ignoring the problem of sin.

31. Anselm, *Why God Became Man* 1.13 (pp. 284–85).

things they suffer, but as Boethius puts it, an even greater and "juster
sympathy is . . . due to those who are guilty. They ought to be brought
to justice not by a prosecution counsel with an air of outrage, but by
a prosecution kind and sympathetic . . . so that their guilt could be
cut back by punishment like a malignant growth"[32]—for the reality
and condition of sin are a horror, a sickness-unto-death. A forgiveness
that ignores sin, that leaves sinners in their sins, is nothing short of
a comprehensive form of torture.

But the answer is far bigger than this—far more comprehensive—
explained not by the evil of sin but by the goodness of God. Forgiveness is indeed an act of mercy, of God's mercy. But as such, "it meets
us, not in spite of, but in and with all the holiness, righteousness
and wisdom of God. It claims us—cleaning, judging and redeeming
us. It is also our true and final consolation. For God Himself is in
it. He reveals His very essence in the streaming forth of his grace."[33]
The action of God's mercy, because it is the action of God himself,
is necessarily an action of holiness, righteousness, and wisdom as
well, for God is one. Anything less would not be mercy at all, for it
would not be God sharing himself with us. In the work of Jesus, specifically his death and resurrection, God is merciful and forgiving.
"For in this action He interposes no less and no other than Himself
for us. With His good will He takes up our cause and responsibility for us in spite of our bad will. In this action He is manifested in
the whole majesty of His being."[34] The foundation of forgiveness is
not merely that of mercy, for mercy by itself is sick, perverted, and
distorted—and "to understand forgiveness we speak not of grace
generally, but of participation with Christ."[35] The foundation of
forgiveness is the whole character of God in relation to sin. The
foundation of forgiveness is God in Christ dealing with our sin so
that we might be free.

32. Boethius, *Consolation of Philosophy*, 100.
33. Barth, *CD* II/2, 356.
34. Barth, *CD* II/2, 356.
35. Coutts, *A Shared Mercy*, 31.

What Forgiveness Is: A Deeper Look

What does it mean for God to forgive (for forgiveness is first and foremost the Lord's, and only secondarily and derivatively our own work)? *Negatively, it means that God in his freedom and love is free not to hold our sin and its consequences directly against us.*[36] Sin has no power and control over God. He, in his freedom, is free with regard to sin—free to choose how to comport himself toward it. But while that may be true, Christianity treads on thin ice when it allows for merely negative definitions or accounts of things, for God is good, his actions are good, and his creative joy is simply too positive to easily allow for merely negative definitions (saying what something is not or what it doesn't do). *Positively, forgiveness is the freedom of God in the face of sin.* "Grace is the distinctive mode of God's being in so far as it seeks and creates fellowship by its own free inclination and favour, unconditioned by any merit or claim in the beloved, but also unhindered by any unworthiness or opposition in the latter."[37] Forgiveness is the opportunity to act "in a manner that is not completely predetermined by previous acts," specifically by past wrongs.[38] Put more expansively, God's forgiveness is the self-giving of God by which he, in his freedom, makes our sin his own in Christ that we might have the corresponding freedom to participate in the merciful, holy, and righteous life of God.[39] Forgiveness is the unique dynamic of *God's freedom before sin*: the freedom to be himself before sin; the freedom not to be forced or constrained

36. While this is similar to J. C. Rutledge's account ("To forgive someone is to no longer count their sins against them"), I think the inclusion of "directly" is important, as a way of acknowledging the fact that God still does attend to or hold sin accountable. Forgiveness is a part of, not the sole concern in, God's dealing with us sinners. The gospel is bigger than the parable of the prodigal son. Rutledge, *Forgiveness and Atonement*, 62.

37. Barth, *CD* II/1, 353. Forgiveness is, as Smyth puts it, "an expression of God's freedom and grace made visible in the life, death, and resurrection of Jesus Christ." Smyth, "Brokenness, Forgiveness, Healing, and Peace in Ireland," 336.

38. Ansorge, "Justice and Mercy," 133.

39. Paul, in Ephesians, "points out the relevance of the work of Christ to the process of forgiveness. Forgiveness in Christ means forgiveness because of all that Christ is and does. Christ died for the forgiveness of his people." Morris, "Forgiveness," 312.

or held hostage by sin,[40] to have limits and conditions and behaviors forced or necessitated by sin; but the freedom for God to be himself, in all that this entails, in the presence of sin, the freedom to give himself to the sinner. God's forgiveness is God's self-giving, that our sin might be fully dealt with, that we genuinely might be freed from sin in Christ and freed to live a life of freedom in him. As such, forgiveness is not simply an act of mercy, of ignoring, bypassing, letting be, or pretending as if things are different than they are.[41] Mercy, on its own, can prolong suffering by refusing to use a scalpel, or it can rush to end suffering with the all-too-ready use of one. Mercy without justice,[42] wisdom, and love is a catastrophic, monstrous, foolish, unjust, and destructive thing. God's forgiveness is an act of God and, therefore, an act of mercy and *everything else that God is*, as God extends himself to us for our well-being, our restored life in him. Forgiveness "meets us, not in spite of, but in and with all the holiness, righteousness and wisdom of God. . . . For God Himself is in it."[43]

For this reason, forgiveness in Scripture does not consist primarily in looking the other way; it is not merely negative—though this may, under certain conditions, be its outer shell, as it were. Forgiveness is the self-giving of God to bring about a genuine freedom from sin in

40. Coutts seems to be quite right when he writes, "Forgiving is free self-giving in the face of sin." Coutts, *A Shared Mercy*, 123.

41. Volf, "Forgiveness, Reconciliation, and Justice," 36. As Allais puts it, "If forgiveness involves ceasing to see a wrong as attaching to a wrongdoer but without changing a judgment about the wrongdoer's culpability and the wrongness of the action, it seems irrational; it seems to involve seeing a person incorrectly. On the other hand, if a change in how you see them is warranted[,] . . . it seems there is nothing more to be done than recognize this: there is nothing more for forgiveness to do" (Allais, "Frailty and Forgiveness," 259). I find this incredibly insightful. The atonement helps us relate to this point in a complex manner. In forgiving, we are acknowledging that something is true of someone that they may or may not know about: that they are forgiven in Christ and that their acceptance of this fact in faith determines their blessedness or damnation. In forgiving them, we are recognizing and embracing the fact of their standing before God, a fact that they may well not be aware of and one that opens new avenues of acting and relating between us.

42. Cf. Hahn and Werner, *Mercy and Justice*; Dalferth and Kimball, *Love and Justice*; Barth, *CD* II/1, 368–466.

43. Barth, *CD* II/1, 356.

all its dimensions: physical, psychological, social, cultic, theological, and so forth. And because of this, it is a matter not merely of volition or of psychological states but of an action—an action of God entering into our lives and taking up the problem in its full reality, that we, participating by faith in the risen Lord, might be free from the power of sin, from the presence of evil in our lives, and free to extend forgiveness to others. It is, as Maximos the Confessor says, "a matter of refusing to stay at the level of the visible world . . . and of aspiring to that which is by nature unassailable"—a matter of recognizing and operating at the level of the kingdom of God.[44] To bring this paragraph full circle, given the nature of divine forgiveness, our forgiveness is *our freedom to be ourselves in Christ in the presence of sin.*[45] For this reason it includes the freedom not to require anything from the perpetrator.[46] There need be no fear of condoning wrongdoing and no lack of self-respect, which might necessitate some precondition in the wrongdoer for forgiveness (though we are free, in wisdom, in love, and with the counsel of others, to make requirements and stipulations). This is a matter of the freedom of God and our freedom in him, to be who we are in Christ toward the sinner. For when God forgives, he does not hold us directly accountable for our sin, but he still deals with the reality and problem of sin in Christ. The forgiveness of God is through the blood of Christ—and our forgiveness is as ones washed by his blood, as members of his body.

"As We Forgive Our Debtors"

What does this understanding of the work of Christ entail for us? Forgiveness, clearly, is not optional for the church. We pray that God

44. Maximos, "On the Lord's Prayer," 301. Cf. McKenny, "Freedom, Responsibility, and Moral Agency," 311.

45. The basis for this reality is the way that God's love is holy, "is characterized by the fact that God, as He seeks and creates fellowship, is always the Lord. He therefore distinguishes and maintains His own will as against every other will. He condemns, excludes and annihilates all contradiction and resistance to it." Barth, *CD* II/1, 359; cf. 360.

46. Warmke, Nelkin, and McKenna, "Forgiveness," 19.

will forgive our debts, "as we also have forgiven our debtors" (Matt.
6:12). But Jesus goes on to say, "For if you forgive others their trespasses, your heavenly Father will also forgive you, but if you do not
forgive others their trespasses, neither will your Father forgive your
trespasses" (6:14–15). Christianity is not merely about freedom from
sin or life in heaven; it is about the freedom to be in Christ, to be
conformed to his image, to be "what the self-emptying of the only-
begotten Son through the flesh has now made us; which shows us
. . . the heights to which we have been raised by his compassionate
hand."[47] God became human that we might participate in the life of
God, might "share in the divine nature (cf. 2 Pet. 1:4)."[48] God forgave
that we might forgive. God forgave, and therefore we must forgive!
But what precisely are we being called to do?

Again, we will begin with negations. First, we are not being called
to repeat the work of Christ. Jesus died once and for all, the perfect
sacrifice for the forgiveness of sins. The church and its members are
not asked to do another work, a work separate from that of Jesus that
is like his and effective like his.[49] We are not to be a second Messiah,
a second Christ. Second, we are not asked to forgive merely in the
sense of pretending that evil has not happened, ignoring the consequences of evil for both perpetrator and victim. This is, if anything,
a demonic form of forgiveness, a parody that ultimately denies the
reality and consequences of sin and, in so doing, allows it to thrive
and prosper. Ultimately, forgiveness may involve forgetting about a
sin or a wrong, or having so much distance from it that the memory
no longer holds any power over us and our relationship with the
wrongdoer whatsoever. But forgiveness is perfectly compatible with
and necessarily entails the affirmation and confession of the reality

47. Maximos, "On the Lord's Prayer," 304.
48. Maximos, "On the Lord's Prayer," 304. Cf. Athanasius, *On the Incarnation* 54 (p. 167).
49. Webster cautions that certain dominant styles of modern theology "emphasize the
coinherence of the divine work of reconciliation and the church's moral action," encouraging
us to ask, "What is the content of the church's ministry of reconciliation, and how is it to
be related to and distinguished from the reconciling act of God in Christ?" Webster, *Word
and Church*, 212–13.

of sin, the pain of its consequences, and the wisdom of dealing with these ongoing realities even in the midst of forgiveness. So again to our question: What precisely are we called to do?

Our understanding begins with the church—the people embracing the forgiveness of God through the passion of Jesus Christ and who have been given participation in the life of God by being cleansed and united to Jesus as members of his body by his Holy Spirit. This is who is commanded to forgive. Forgiveness is a work we do *as members of his body*: we extend the forgiveness of Jesus to others; we witness to the mystery of his forgiveness by being the outward sign and manifestation of his work.[50] "His action forgives sin, the church's does not," for the latter is a "repetition of the judgment of God which is established at the cross and resurrection from which the new creation comes."[51] Given this view, to refuse to forgive is to exclude oneself from the forgiveness of God, for it is to separate oneself from Jesus and his work.[52] The following three points unpack aspects of this fundamental thesis.

First, it means that the person forgiving has their fundamental identity in being a member of the church: of being forgiven by God through the passion and resurrection of Jesus, of being given participation in the life of God by being cleansed and united to Jesus as a member of his body by his Holy Spirit. The abuse and its consequences are not to be denied, but far less are we to deny the honor, dignity, and worth that come from being forgiven and restored by Jesus, from being a member of his body.[53] We do not ultimately forgive on the basis of

50. Webster, *Word and Church*, 222. Cf. Habets: "Our response of faith and repentance is a participation in a response already made by the incarnate Son"—the same being true of our extension of forgiveness to others. Habets, "'To Err Is Human, to Forgive Is Divine,'" 13.

51. Webster, *Word and Church*, 221.

52. Ellingworth, "Forgiveness of Sins," 242.

53. Cf. Springhart, "'. . . As We Forgive Those Who Trespass against Us . . . '?," 161–68. Concluding, Springhart writes, "If forgiveness is understood as a process, then a justification that has already been granted plays an important constitutive factor. The Christological reason for this lies in the vicarious salvation of Christ on the cross. Here it becomes apparent that human beings in the abundance of life are just and sinful at the same time. This means that human beings are both perpetrators *and* victims," and for this reason we cannot divide

or from the perspective of our victimhood, though when we do so, it can be powerful: "I have looked into the abyss of human evil," writes Archbishop Desmond Tutu. "You encounter people who, having suffered grievously, should by right have been riddled with bitterness and a lust for revenge and retribution. But they are different."[54] And what is this difference? It is not something we do primarily in order to find healing and peace or to deal with the dynamics of our suffering (though such healing and coping may indeed occur); those united to Christ and forgiven by him witness to God's forgiveness by extending it to others. The distinction is a matter of the power and resources from which forgiveness flows.[55] While being a victim may serve as the occasion for forgiveness—a prerequisite, we might say, or the circumstances within which the dynamics of forgiveness can unfold and apart from which they would not make sense—it is the victim's identity in Christ as a forgiven one that shapes and empowers their forgiveness, for "truthful human action is action which is in conformity with the reality which is established in the resurrection of Jesus from the dead."[56] I forgive not because I am a victim but because I am forgiven. "There is a defined freedom from whence forgiveness comes, and it is a definition that is provided by neither the victim nor the offender."[57] The Christian tradition "sees all people as marred by evil," and it "rejects the construction of the world around exclusive moral polarities—here, on our side, 'the just, the pure, the innocent,' and there, on the other side, 'the unjust, the defiled, the guilty.' Such an exclusively polarized world does not exist."[58] To forgive is not primarily to affirm my identity as a victim. We are called to affirm our

people into groups of *either* victims *or* perpetrators. Put succinctly, there are deeper levels of personhood, constituted by Christ, than being a victim and/or perpetrator.

54. Tutu, foreword to *Forgiveness and Reconciliation*, xi.
55. Petersen, "Theology of Forgiveness," 15.
56. Webster, *Word and Church*, 224.
57. Coutts, *A Shared Mercy*, 121–22.
58. Volf, "Forgiveness, Reconciliation, and Justice," 42. As Lippitt puts it, the "consciousness of one's sin is not about 'particulars'—*this particular* sin—but about recognizing one's whole self as sinful and corrupt." Lippitt, *Love's Forgiveness*, 68.

identity, worth, and honor in Christ as members of his body—and on that basis, to relate to the sins of others against us.[59]

Second, forgiveness is not something the victim does alone. The person in question is who he or she is in Christ and, therefore, is a member of the people forgiven by and united in him.[60] One who has suffered wrong forgives as a part of this people and, therefore, with their support, guidance, and resources. While circumstances may unfold such that we suffer or forgive in physical isolation from the church, forgiveness is something we do as a member of that people whether they are present or not, and under normal circumstances, it is something we do in the physical presence and tangible support of that people. Forgiveness puts victims in a position not of weakness but of strength: of sharing what they have received in the company of others who have received it as well. The power of the perpetrator lies, more often than not, in isolation and fear. The true power of forgiveness lies in belonging and safety. When the church calls its members to enact forgiveness as individuals, in isolation, as though forgiveness were a merely personal matter, it fails in its calling, to the danger and harm of its members. We are called to confess sin, expose sin,[61] to bring others into the dynamics of understanding, dealing with, and ultimately forgiving sin, so that forgiveness may be a corporate work.

Third, forgiveness is a matter of self-giving in mercy and, therefore, giving far more than mere mercy. Mercy is God's giving from his own divine abundance to creatures in need. Our need is the occasion for mercy but not its cause; "its cause is simply the incomparable, ceaseless goodness of God."[62] But we in Christ can and should likewise

---

59. This, I take it, is the ultimate basis for self-esteem or self-respect that is genuinely connected to resentment. Cf. Lippitt, *Love's Forgiveness*, 1–40, especially 16.

60. McKenny's unpacking of Bonhoeffer's thought on freedom, responsibility, and moral agency is quite helpful here. See McKenny, "Freedom, Responsibility, and Moral Agency."

61. Forgiveness is forgiveness of sin and therefore a full recognition, judgment, and protest against it. Forgiveness does not reject "blaming emotions," because it is part of a larger picture that honors and deals with them. Shoemaker, "The Forgiven," 43.

62. Webster, *God without Measure*, 2:55.

give from the abundance we have in him. As we extend ourselves to others, we extend Christ to others, for we are his body, and he is our blessing, our abundance. And to extend true mercy, the mercy of God, is far more than adopting a neutral posture, a state in which we release resentment or negative emotion[63] or act as though wrong has not occurred. To extend mercy is to extend wisdom, justice, love, and holiness as well, and to do so freely, joyfully. And this is a fearful thing. Doctors know what it entails to be merciful: it is not to refrain from causing pain, to act as though a wound were not there, or to act as if a tumor were not malignant. Sometimes (recall the introduction), for a doctor to be merciful is for them to extend wisdom and goodness to the body in the form of cutting, wounding, scraping, amputating, or bringing the body to the point of death or even just beyond it in the hopes of bringing about health and well-being.

As a self-giving act, forgiveness says to the sinner, "I release my claim on your sin, my anger and hatred, my need for vengeance"— but it doesn't stop there![64] It goes on to say, "I refuse to relate to you and your sin on the basis of our history alone. I relate to you freely, as one who is forgiven by Christ, and I relate to you as one to whom Christ extends forgiveness. And because I relate to you on this basis, I seek to extend to you the whole character of God as I am called to image it." Forgiveness means that we extend wisdom in dealing with the complex spiritual, physical, mental, and social dynamics of sin in the sinner. It means that we invite them into truth and, therefore, into confession—perhaps corporate or public confession and the social and judiciary consequences this may entail—for "negation is constitutive of forgiveness. To offer forgiveness is at the same time to condemn the deed and accuse the doer."[65] It means that we invite

63. Lippitt, *Love's Forgiveness*, 10–12; F. Rutledge, *The Crucifixion*, 73. By saying that forgiveness is more than this, I do not mean to reject the role of both releasing and affirming negative emotions within forgiveness. Rather, I want to situate them within a larger framework.

64. Whether forgiveness should involve meeting in person with the one being forgiven is a question to be discerned by the church, with due attention to the relevant dangers and power dynamics involved.

65. Volf, "Forgiveness, Reconciliation, and Justice," 45.

them into justice—a dynamic that can and should at times involve restitution[66] and/or punishment, for punishment is the bastion and support of law.[67] Forgiveness means, in short, that we invite the sinner, in many ways, into the pain and vulnerability of healing in Christ.

What does it mean for a victim to extend the mercy of forgiveness to a perpetrator? It means that they—on the basis of their identity in Christ, what he has offered them, and their membership in his body, and therefore on the basis of the strength and resources of the community and the Spirit that unites it—extend to the perpetrator what they have received in Christ: the merciful self-giving of God that not only puts aside their sin by bearing it but invites them into the honor, purity, and love that is the life of God. It is not something we do merely out of weakness or need, in an effort to find healing or to avoid addressing conflict appropriately. Far from it! It is rather an extension of the strength and healing we have in Christ, which we, on that basis, can extend to those who have harmed us. (To "love your neighbor as yourself," we can add, "love as you have been loved.") The deeper meaning of forgiveness is that of giving: Christ giving himself for us and our giving of ourselves for others—a work we do in him and with those who are with us in him.[68]

A danger attends this thought, hinging on a key distinction. Is the forgiveness we extend an imitation of Christ's forgiveness, or are we in some sense participating in, extending, or manifesting the forgiveness of Christ to others? The answer is yes—but the devil is in the details (as are the angels). When we are acting, we are extending real forgiveness, and the work is similar to that of Christ, an imitation. We are taking up "our" cross and following him (Luke 9:23). Should we leave it at that, however, things become precarious. I was present when the elders of a church (not my own) told one of my

66. Swinburne, "Forgiving as a Performative Utterance," 137.

67. Allais, "Frailty and Forgiveness," 268. Cf. Lippitt, *Love's Forgiveness*, 26–27, 124–25; F. Rutledge, *The Crucifixion*, 76–77.

68. Note the "gift" language in the earliest meanings of *forgive* in the *Oxford English Dictionary*.

students that she should imitate Christ by staying in an abusive situation because good might come of it. I had read of such things, of course, but had never seen anything like it with my own eyes (and hope to never see it again). The danger is that we seek to become another Christ or that we call others to do so, as though Jesus does his work, and we do ours—a form of idolatry in which we take up the burden of being another Christ. Our calling is to extend the mind and Spirit of Christ into the chaos around us, witnessing to others and extending to them the work that he has done for us all. But we do this as his body.[69] We do this as the church. Ours is a calling not to be a savior but to be in him.

I learned this lesson from literature, particularly Tolkien's *The Lord of the Rings* and Dickens's *A Tale of Two Cities*. Who represents Christ in these two works? Aragorn, a man of no repute, riding the paths of the dead to reclaim his kingdom? Frodo, bearing the burden of Middle Earth? Gandalf, the opponent of Sauron, falling into darkness at the hands of the Balrog? And what of Dickens? Sydney Carton's sacrifice? Lucie's life-giving touch to all around her? Miss Pross, the faithful servant battling to the death to save her family? Literature cannot, in the end, do full justice to the work of Christ by consolidating it into the life and work of a single character, and neither can we. The work of Christ is simply unique and unrepeatable, a work of such density, of such complexity, that only one who is fully God and fully Israelite is able to do it. For literature to do justice to the work of Christ, it must disperse it across a host of characters for the simple reason that Jesus accomplishes his work by means of his body, and his body is now the Spirit-filled church. Our calling as the people of God is to be the body of Christ, to witness to his saving work in thought, word, and deed as we are remade in the image of Christ and therefore live and act in a manner that witnesses to him and extends him and his love to those around us. We are not to repeat but to extend

69. McKenny explores this dynamic in Bonhoeffer's thought. See McKenny, "Freedom, Responsibility, and Moral Agency," 315–20.

a tangible manifestation, a parable or sacrament, of his work, and to do so with the collective resources of the church.

Summary

So what does it mean to say, "I forgive you"?

It means that we say, "I refuse to relate to you on the basis of the way that you wronged me. You did hurt me, and I live with your action's consequences. But my identity is greater than that. I relate to you as one loved by the triune God, as one whose sins are forgiven, and as one who lives in the power of the Holy Spirit and therefore as a member of his church. I relate to you on the basis of the riches I have in Christ."

Because of this we say, "I am free to relate to you in a way that is not constrained by your sin. I am free to release my anger, to relinquish any claims I might have to punishment or restitution. I am free not merely to ignore or to tolerate you but to relate to you with the mind of Christ in love, wisdom, justice, holiness, and so forth."

But the "I" in question must be specified: "I am free as a member of the church and therefore as one who is loved and supported by a real, tangible community, one who does not forgive alone but as a member of a fellowship, some of whom know my story, know of your wrong, and can support and love both of us in dealing with its consequences. I am free to forgive because I belong, I am supported, and I am part of a membership that protects me from the isolation and vulnerability common to victims."

And because we are free in these ways, it means that we can say, "I forgive you whether you recognize your sin or not. I forgive you, but I am free to discern whether it is wise for me to reenter some kind of relationship with you or not. I forgive you, but it may still be good or wise for me to press charges against you or otherwise seek some kind of punishment or imprisonment for you, for your benefit or that of others."

What is the root of all this? It is God's freedom in relation to sin. The freedom not to be forced by sin to act in a certain way. The freedom to relate to it, to judge and destroy it. But the freedom to do so in himself, by bearing our sin in Jesus Christ. And therefore, ultimately, the freedom to give us himself, that we may be like him, that we may be in his image, that we may be free.

Worship

Mark 11:25 tells us, "And when you stand praying, if you hold anything against anyone, forgive them, so that your Father in heaven may forgive you your sins" (NIV). To rephrase: when you stand ready to worship, "if you hold anything against anyone, forgive them, so that your Father in heaven may forgive you your sins"—and then worship. Why? Because God wants to be worshiped not merely with the right words but with the right actions. And the right actions have to do with our holistic conformity to Christ in the power of the Holy Spirit. Not only are we to read and study theology, not only are we to think rightly about who God is and what he has done; we are to obey him. We are to forgive as we have been forgiven; we are to extend the forgiveness of Christ to others. And that will be a significant part of our worship—and an entry point to a yet richer theology.

DOXOLOGICAL POSTLUDE

Calvin's Institutes

We see that our whole salvation and all its parts are comprehended in Christ [Acts 4:12]. We should therefore take care not to derive the least portion of it from anywhere else. If we seek salvation, we are taught by the very name of Jesus that it is "of him" [1 Cor. 1:30]. If we seek any other gifts of the Spirit, they will be found in his anointing. If we seek strength, it lies in his dominion; if purity, in his conception; if gentleness, it appears in his birth. For by his birth he was made like us in all respects [Heb. 2:17] that he might learn to feel our pain [cf. Heb. 5:2]. If we seek redemption, it lies in his passion; if acquittal, in his condemnation; if remission of the curse, in his cross [Gal. 3:13]; if satisfaction, in his sacrifice; if purification, in his blood; if reconciliation, in his descent into hell; if mortification of the flesh, in his tomb; if newness of life, in his resurrection; if immortality, in the same; if inheritance of the Heavenly Kingdom, in his entrance into heaven; if protection, if security, if abundant supply of all blessings, in his Kingdom; if untroubled expectation of judgment, in the power given to him to judge. In short, since rich store of every kind of good abounds in him, let us drink our fill from this fountain, and from no other.[1]

1. Calvin, *Institutes* II.xvi.19 (pp. 527–28).

Bibliography

Abelard, Peter. *Commentary on the Epistle to the Romans*. Translated by Steven R. Cartwright. FC. Washington, DC: Catholic University of America Press, 2011.

Ables, Travis E. *The Body of the Cross: Holy Victims and the Invention of the Atonement*. New York: Fordham University Press, 2022.

Adams, Marilyn McCord. *Christ and Horrors: The Coherence of Christology*. Cambridge: Cambridge University Press, 2006.

Allais, Lucy. "Frailty and Forgiveness: Forgiveness for Humans." In Warmke, Nelkin, and McKenna, *Forgiveness and Its Moral Dimensions*, 257–84.

Anderson, Gary A. *That I May Dwell among Them: Incarnation and Atonement in the Tabernacle Narrative*. Grand Rapids: Eerdmans, 2023.

Anselm. *The Major Works*. Edited by Brian Davies and G. R. Evans. New York: Oxford University Press, 1998.

———. "Meditation I: A Meditation to Stir Up Fear." In Anselm, *Prayers and Meditations of Saint Anselm*, 221–24.

———. "On the Procession of the Holy Spirit." In Anselm, *Major Works*, 390–434.

———. *The Prayers and Meditations of Saint Anselm with the Proslogion*. Translated by Benedicta Ward. New York: Penguin, 1973.

———. *Why God Became Man*. In Anselm, *Major Works*, 260–356.

Ansorge, Dirk. "Justice and Mercy: Can They Be Reconciled from a Systematic Point of View?" In Hahn and Werner, *Mercy and Justice*, 123–39.

Athanasius. *The Letters of Saint Athanasius concerning the Holy Spirit*. Translated by C. R. B. Shapland. London: Epworth, 1951.

————. *On the Incarnation*. Translated by John Behr. Popular Patristics 44A. Yonkers, NY: St. Vladimir's Seminary Press, 2011.

Augustine. *The Augustine Catechism: The Enchiridion on Faith, Hope, and Charity*. Translated by Bruce Harbert. Hyde Park, NY: New City, 1999.

————. *The City of God against the Pagans*. Translated by R. W. Dyson. New York: Cambridge University Press, 1998.

————. *Confessions*. Translated by Henry Chadwick. Oxford: Oxford University Press, 1991.

————. *Expositions of the Psalms 1–32*. Translated by Maria Boulding. WSA III/15. Hyde Park, NY: New City, 2000.

————. *Expositions of the Psalms 33–50*. Translated by Maria Boulding. WSA III/16. Hyde Park, NY: New City, 2000.

————. *Expositions of the Psalms 73–98*. Translated by Maria Boulding. WSA HI/18. Hyde Park, NY: New City, 2001.

————. *Expositions of the Psalms 99–120*. Translated by Maria Boulding. WSA III/19. Hyde Park, NY: New City, 2004.

————. *Sermons (51–94): On the New Testament*. Translated by Edmund Hill. WSA III/3. New Rochelle, NY: New City, 1992.

————. *Sermons (184–229z): On the Liturgical Seasons*. WSA III/6. New Rochelle, NY: New City, 1993.

————. *Sermons (230–72): On the Liturgical Seasons*. WSA III/7. New Rochelle, NY: New City, 1993.

————. *Sermons (341–400): On Various Subjects*. WSA III/10. New Rochelle, NY: New City, 2009.

————. *The Trinity*. Translated by Edmund Hill. WSA I/5. Brooklyn, NY: New City, 1991.

Aulén, Gustaf. *Christus Victor: An Historical Study of the Three Main Types of the Idea of Atonement*. Translated by A. G. Hebert. New York: Macmillan, 1951.

Balthasar, Hans Urs von. *Mysterium Paschale: The Mystery of Easter*. Translated by Aidan Nichols. San Francisco: Ignatius, 1990.

————. *Theo-Drama: Theological Dramatic Theory*. Vol. 4, *The Action*. Translated by Graham Harrison. San Francisco: Ignatius, 1988.

Barker, P. A. "Sabbath, Sabbatical Year, Jubilee." In *Dictionary of the Old Testament: Pentateuch*, edited by T. Desmond Alexander and David W. Baker, 695–706. Downers Grove, IL: InterVarsity, 2003.

Barth, Karl. *Church Dogmatics*. Translated by G. W. Bromiley and T. F. Torrance. 14 vols. Edinburgh: T&T Clark, 1936–77.

———. *Dogmatics in Outline*. Translated by G. T. Thompson. New York: Harper, 1959.

———. *Protestant Theology in the Nineteenth Century: Its Background and History*. Translated by Brian Cozens and John Bowden. New ed. Grand Rapids: Eerdmans, 2002.

Basil the Great. *On the Holy Spirit*. Translated by Stephen M. Hildebrand. Popular Patristics 42. New York: St. Vladimir's Seminary Press, 2011.

Baur, Ferdinand Christian. *History of Christian Dogma*. Translated by Robert F. Brown and Peter C. Hodgson. Oxford: Oxford University Press, 2014.

Bauspiess, Martin, Christof Landmesser, and David Lincicum, eds. *Ferdinand Christian Baur and the History of Early Christianity*. Translated by Robert F. Brown and Peter C. Hodgson. Oxford: Oxford University Press, 2017.

Bavinck, Herman. *Reformed Dogmatics*. Vol. 3, *Sin and Salvation in Christ*. Edited by John Bolt. Translated by John Vriend. Grand Rapids: Baker Academic, 2006.

Beale, G. K. *The Temple and the Church's Mission: A Biblical Theology of the Dwelling Place of God*. Downers Grove, IL: InterVarsity, 2004.

Behr, John. *The Mystery of Christ: Life in Death*. Crestwood, NY: St. Vladimir's Seminary Press, 2006.

Bellinger, William H., Jr., and William R. Farmer, eds. *Jesus and the Suffering Servant: Isaiah 53 and Christian Origins*. 1998. Reprint, Eugene, OR: Wipf & Stock, 2009.

Bird, Michael, and Scott Harrower, eds. *Unlimited Atonement: Amyraldism and Reformed Theology*. Grand Rapids: Kregel Academic, 2023.

Block, Daniel I. *The Book of Ezekiel*. 2 vols. NICOT. Grand Rapids: Eerdmans, 1997–98.

Blowers, Paul M. *Maximus the Confessor: Jesus Christ and the Transfiguration of the World*. Oxford: Oxford University Press, 2016.

Boersma, Hans. *Scripture as Real Presence: Sacramental Exegesis in the Early Church*. Grand Rapids: Baker Academic, 2017.

Boethius. *The Consolation of Philosophy*. Translated by V. E. Watts. New York: Penguin, 1999.

Bonaventure. *Breviloquium*. Translated by Dominic Monti. St. Bonaventure, NY: Franciscan Institute, 2005.

———. "The Tree of Life." In *Bonaventure: The Soul's Journey into God, the Tree of Life, the Life of St. Francis*, translated by Ewert Cousins, 117–75. CWS. New York: Paulist Press, 1994.

Bonino, Serge-Thomas. *Reading the Song of Songs with St. Thomas Aquinas*. Translated by Andrew Levering. Washington, DC: Catholic University of America Press, 2023.

Bosworth, F. F. *Christ the Healer: Sermons on Divine Healing*. 1924. Reprint, New Kensington, PA: Whitaker House, 2000.

Brown, Raymond E. *The Death of the Messiah: From Gethsemane to the Grave; A Commentary on the Passion Narratives in the Four Gospels*. 2 vols. New York: Doubleday, 1994.

Bulgakov, Sergius. *The Comforter*. Translated by Boris Jakim. Grand Rapids: Eerdmans, 2004.

Burns, J. Patout. "The Concept of Satisfaction in Medieval Redemption Theory." *Theological Studies* 36 (June 1975): 285–304.

———. "How Christ Saves: Augustine's Multiple Explanations." In *Tradition and the Rule of Faith in the Early Church: Essays in Honor of Joseph T. Lienhard*, edited by Ronnie J. Rombs and Alexander Y. Hwang, 193–210. Washington, DC: Catholic University of America Press, 2010.

Burroughs, John. *The Art of Seeing Things: Essays by John Burroughs*. Edited by Charlotte Zoë Walker. Syracuse: Syracuse University Press, 2001.

Calvin, John. *Commentaries on the Epistle of Paul the Apostle to the Romans*. Translated by John Owen. Reprint, Grand Rapids: Baker, 1979.

———. *Institutes of the Christian Religion*. Translated by Ford Lewis Battles. Philadelphia: Westminster, 1960.

Castelo, Daniel. "Holy Spirit." In *The New Cambridge Companion to Christian Doctrine*, edited by Michael Allen, 103–18. Cambridge: Cambridge University Press, 2023.

Cave, Alfred. "XII." In *The Atonement in Modern Religious Thought: A Theological Symposium*, by Fréderic Godet et al., 239–56. New York: Thomas Whittaker, 1901.

Chazelle, Celia. *The Crucified God in the Carolingian Era: Theology and Art of Christ's Passion*. Cambridge: Cambridge University Press, 2001.

Chilcote, Paul W. *A Faith That Sings: Biblical Themes in the Lyrical Theology of Charles Wesley*. Eugene, OR: Cascade Books, 2016.

Christensen, Michael J., and Jeffery A. Wittung, eds. *Partakers of the Divine Nature: The History and Development of Deification in the Christian Traditions*. Grand Rapids: Baker Academic, 2007.

Clancy, Finbarr G. "Redemption." In *Augustine through the Ages: An Encyclopedia*, edited by Allan D. Fitzgerald, 702–4. Grand Rapids: Eerdmans, 1999.

Cochrane, Arthur C. *Reformed Confessions of the 16th Century*. Philadelphia: Westminster, 1966.

Cocksworth, Ashley. "Prayer." In Johnson, *T&T Clark Companion to Atonement*, 701–6.

Cole, Graham A. *God the Peacemaker: How Atonement Brings Shalom*. Downers Grove, IL: InterVarsity, 2009.

Collett, Don. "Book of the Twelve." In Johnson, *T&T Clark Companion to Atonement*, 411–16.

Coutts, Jon. *A Shared Mercy: Karl Barth on Forgiveness and the Church*. Downers Grove, IL: InterVarsity, 2016.

Craig, William Lane. *Atonement and the Death of Christ: An Exegetical, Historical, and Philosophical Exploration*. Waco: Baylor University Press, 2020.

Crisp, Oliver D. *Participation and Atonement: An Analytic and Constructive Account*. Grand Rapids: Baker Academic, 2022.

Crisp, Oliver D., and Fred Sanders, eds. *Locating Atonement: Explorations in Constructive Dogmatics*. Grand Rapids: Zondervan, 2015.

Cyril of Alexandria. *Glaphyra on the Pentateuch*. Vol. 1, *Genesis*. Translated by Nicholas P. Lunn. FC. Washington, DC: Catholic University of America Press, 2018.

———. *On the Unity of Christ*. Translated by John Anthony McGuckin. Crestwood, NY: St. Vladimir's Seminary Press, 1995.

Cyril of Jerusalem. *The Works of Saint Cyril of Jerusalem*. Vol. 1. Translated by Leo P. McCauley and Anthony A. Stephenson. FC. Washington, DC: Catholic University of America Press, 1969.

Dales, Douglas. *Alcuin: Theology and Thought*. Cambridge: James Clarke, 2013.

Dalferth, Ingolf U., and Trevor W. Kimball, eds. *Love and Justice: Consonance or Dissonance?* Tübingen: Mohr Siebeck, 2019.

Dante Alighieri. *Inferno*. Translated by Anthony Esolen. New York: Random House, 2003.

Dauphinais, Michael, Andrew Hofer, and Roger W. Nutt, eds. *Thomas Aquinas and the Greek Fathers*. Washington, DC: Catholic University of America Press, 2018.

Dawson, John. "Hatred's End: A Christian Proposal to Peacemaking in a New Century." In Helmick and Petersen, *Forgiveness and Reconciliation*, 229–54.

Dorner, I. A. *A System of Christian Doctrine*. Translated by Alfred Cave and J. S. Banks. 4 vols. Edinburgh: T&T Clark, 1880.

Duby, Stephen J. *Jesus and the God of Classical Theism: Biblical Christology in Light of the Doctrine of God*. Grand Rapids: Baker Academic, 2022.

Dunn, James D. G. *Baptism in the Holy Spirit.* Naperville, IL: Allenson, 1970.

Edwards, Jonathan. *The Religious Affections.* Edinburgh: Banner of Truth Trust, 1986.

———. "The Wisdom of God Displayed in the Way of Salvation." In *The Works of Jonathan Edwards,* edited by Henry Rogers, Sereno Edwards Dwight, and Edward Hickman, 2:141–56. Peabody, MA: Hendrickson, 1998.

Ellingworth, Paul. "Forgiveness of Sins." In *Dictionary of Jesus and the Gospels,* edited by Joel B. Green, Scot McKnight, and I. Howard Marshall, 241–43. Downers Grove, IL: InterVarsity, 1992.

Emerson, Matthew Y. *"He Descended to the Dead": An Evangelical Theology of Holy Saturday.* Downers Grove, IL: IVP Academic, 2019.

Farrow, Douglas. *Ascension Theology.* London: T&T Clark, 2011.

Fletcher-Louis, Crispin. "The High Priest in Ben Sira 50." In *Atonement: Jewish and Christian Origins,* edited by Max Botner, Justin Harrison Duff, and Simon Dürr, 89–111. Grand Rapids: Eerdmans, 2020.

Franks, Robert S. *A History of the Doctrine of the Work of Christ in Its Ecclesiastical Development.* Vol. 1. London: Hodder & Stoughton, 1871.

Gavrilyuk, Paul L. "God's Impassible Suffering in the Flesh: The Promise of Paradoxical Christology." In *Divine Impassibility and the Mystery of Human Suffering,* edited by James F. Keating and Thomas Joseph White, 127–49. Grand Rapids: Eerdmans, 2009.

Gorman, Michael J. *The Death of the Messiah and the Birth of the New Covenant: A (Not So) New Model of the Atonement.* Eugene, OR: Cascade Books, 2014.

Graham, Jeannine Michele. "Substitution and Representation." In Johnson, *T&T Clark Companion to Atonement,* 763–68.

Graves, Michael. "Exodus." In *The Oxford Handbook of Early Christian Biblical Interpretation,* edited by Paul M. Blowers and Peter W. Martens, 547–60. Oxford: Oxford University Press, 2019.

Gregory of Nazianzus. "Epistle CI." *NPNF*[2] 7:439–43.

———. *On God and Christ.* Translated by Frederick Williams and Lionel Wickham. Popular Patristics 23. Crestwood, NY: St. Vladimir's Seminary Press, 2002.

Gregory of Nyssa. *An Address on Religious Instruction.* In *Christology of the Later Fathers,* edited by Edward R. Hardy, 268–325. Philadelphia: Westminster, 1954.

Gregory the Great. *Moralia in Job.* Translated by James Bliss and Charles Marriott. 3 vols. Jackson, MI: Ex Fontibus, 2012.

Grosseteste, Robert. *On the Cessation of the Laws*. Translated by Stephen M. Hildebrand. FC. Washington, DC: Catholic University of America Press, 2012.

Habets, Myk. "'To Err Is Human, to Forgive Is Divine': The Ontological Foundations of Forgiveness." In *The Art of Forgiveness*, edited by Philip Halstead and Myk Habets, 3–16. Minneapolis: Fortress, 2018.

Hahn, Judith, and Gunda Werner, eds. *Mercy and Justice: A Challenge for Contemporary Theology*. Leiden: Brill, 2020.

Harnack, Adolf von. "Atonement." In *The Atonement in Modern Religious Thought: A Theological Symposium*, by Fréderic Godet et al., 3–20. New York: Thomas Whittaker, 1901.

———. *What Is Christianity?* New York: Harper, 1957.

Hart, Trevor A. "Irenaeus, Recapitulation and Physical Redemption." In *Christ in Our Place: The Humanity of God in Christ for the Reconciliation of the World*, edited by Trevor A. Hart and Daniel P. Thimell, 152–81. Allison Park, PA: Pickwick, 1989.

Hauke, Manfred. *Introduction to Mariology*. Translated by Richard Chonak. Washington, DC: Catholic University of America Press, 2008.

Hegel, G. W. F. *Lectures on the Philosophy of Religion: The Lectures of 1827*. Translated by Peter C. Hodgson and Robert F. Brown. New York: Clarendon, 2006.

Helmick, Raymond G., and Rodney L. Petersen, eds. *Forgiveness and Reconciliation: Religion, Public Policy, and Conflict Transformation*. Philadelphia: Templeton Foundation, 2001.

Heppe, Heinrich. *Reformed Dogmatics: Set Out and Illustrated from the Sources*. Translated by G. T. Thomson. London: Allen & Unwin, 1950.

Herbert, George. "The Sacrifice." In *The Complete English Poems*, edited by John Tobin, 23–30. New York: Penguin, 1991.

Hill, Charles E., and Frank A. James, eds. *The Glory of the Atonement: Biblical, Historical and Practical Perspectives*. Downers Grove, IL: InterVarsity, 2004.

Hodge, Charles. *Systematic Theology*. Vol. 2. Grand Rapids: Eerdmans, 1986.

Hogg, David S. *Anselm of Canterbury: The Beauty of Theology*. Burlington, VT: Ashgate, 2004.

Holmes, Christopher R. J. "The Atonement and the Holy Spirit." In Johnson, *T&T Clark Companion to Atonement*, 77–94.

Holmes, Michael W. *The Apostolic Fathers in English*. 3rd ed. Grand Rapids: Baker Academic, 2006.

Holmes, Stephen R. "Penal Substitution." In Johnson, *T&T Clark Companion to Atonement*, 295–314.

Hooker, Richard. *Of the Laws of Ecclesiastical Polity*. 2 vols. New York: Dutton, 1954.

Horton, Michael. *Rediscovering the Holy Spirit: God's Perfecting Presence in Creation, Redemption, and Everyday Life*. Grand Rapids: Zondervan, 2017.

Hoskins, Paul M. *Jesus as the Fulfillment of the Temple in the Gospel of John*. Milton Keynes, UK: Paternoster, 2006.

Howard, Thomas Albert. *Protestant Theology and the Making of the Modern German University*. Oxford: Oxford University Press, 2006.

Irenaeus. *Against Heresies. ANF* 1:309–567.

Jamieson, R. B., and Tyler R. Wittman. *Biblical Reasoning: Christological and Trinitarian Rules for Exegesis*. Grand Rapids: Baker Academic, 2022.

Janowski, Bernd, and Peter Stuhlmacher. *The Suffering Servant: Isaiah 53 in Jewish and Christian Sources*. Grand Rapids: Eerdmans, 2004.

Jenson, Robert W. *Systematic Theology*. Vol. 1, *The Triune God*. Oxford: Oxford University Press, 1997.

John of Damascus. *Exposition of the Orthodox Faith*. Translated by S. D. F. Salmond. Grand Rapids: Eerdmans, 1983.

Johnson, Adam. *Atonement: A Guide for the Perplexed*. New York: T&T Clark, 2015.

———. "Barth and Boethius on *Stellvertretung* and Personhood." In *Being Saved: Explorations in Human Salvation*, edited by Marc Cortez, Joshua R. Farris, and S. Mark Hamilton, 201–17. London: SCM, 2018.

———. "A Fuller Account: The Role of 'Fittingness' in Thomas Aquinas' Development of the Doctrine of the Atonement." *International Journal of Systematic Theology* 12, no. 3 (2010): 302–18.

———. *God's Being in Reconciliation: The Theological Basis of the Unity and Diversity of the Atonement in the Theology of Karl Barth*. New York: T&T Clark, 2012.

———. "Peter Abelard." In Johnson, *T&T Clark Companion to Atonement*, 357–60.

———. *The Reconciling Wisdom of God: Reframing the Doctrine of the Atonement*. Bellingham, WA: Lexham, 2016.

———, ed. *T&T Clark Companion to Atonement*. New York: T&T Clark, 2017.

———. "A Temple Framework of the Atonement." *Journal of the Evangelical Theological Society* 54, no. 2 (2011): 225–37.

Johnson, Adam J., and Tessa Hayashida. "The Spirit of the Atonement: The Role of the Holy Spirit in Christ's Death and Resurrection." *Religions* 13, no. 10 (2022): 1–12.

Jones, Paul Dafydd. "The Fury of Love: Calvin on the Atonement." In Johnson, *T&T Clark Companion to Atonement*, 213–36.

Julian of Norwich. *Showings*. Translated by Edmund Colledge and James Walsh. CWS. New York: Paulist Press, 1978.

Justin Martyr. *Dialogue with Trypho*. ANF 1:194–270.

———. *The First and Second Apologies*. Translated by Leslie William Barnard. Ancient Christian Writers. New York: Paulist Press, 1997.

Kant, Immanuel. *Religion within the Boundaries of Mere Reason*. Translated by Allen W. Wood and George Di Giovanni. New York: Cambridge University Press, 1998.

Keating, James F., and Thomas Joseph White. *Divine Impassibility and the Mystery of Human Suffering*. Grand Rapids: Eerdmans, 2009.

Kharlamov, Vladimir, ed. *Theosis: Deification in Christian Theology*. Vol. 2. Eugene, OR: Pickwick, 2011.

Kimbrough, S. T. *The Lyrical Theology of Charles Wesley: A Reader*. Eugene, OR: Cascade Books, 2013.

Lane, Anthony N. S. *Bernard of Clairvaux: Theologian of the Cross*. Collegeville, MN: Cistercian Publications, 2013.

———. "The Wrath of God as an Aspect of the Love of God." In *Nothing Greater, Nothing Better: Theological Essays on the Love of God*, edited by Kevin J. Vanhoozer, 138–67. Grand Rapids: Eerdmans, 2001.

Lanfranc of Canterbury. *On the Body and Blood of the Lord*. Translated by Mark G. Vaillancourt. FC. Washington, DC: Catholic University of America Press, 2009.

Lauber, David. *Barth on the Descent into Hell: God, Atonement and the Christian Life*. Burlington, VT: Ashgate, 2004.

Leithart, Peter J. *Delivered from the Elements of the World: Atonement, Justification, Mission*. Downers Grove, IL: InterVarsity, 2016.

Leontius of Byzantium. *Contra Aphthartodocetas*. In *Complete Works*, translated by Brian E. Daley, 336–409. Oxford: Oxford University Press, 2017.

Levering, Matthew. *Christ's Fulfillment of Torah and Temple: Salvation according to Thomas Aquinas*. Notre Dame, IN: University of Notre Dame Press, 2002.

Lewis, Alan E. *Between Cross and Resurrection: A Theology of Holy Saturday*. Grand Rapids: Eerdmans, 2001.

Lewis, C. S. Preface to *On the Incarnation*, by Athanasius, 9–15. Translated by John Behr. Popular Patristics 44A. Yonkers, NY: St. Vladimir's Seminary Press, 2011.

Lippitt, John. *Love's Forgiveness: Kierkegaard, Resentment, Humility, and Hope.* Oxford: Oxford University Press, 2020.

Lombard, Peter. *The Sentences.* Vol. 3. Translated by Giulio Silano. Toronto: Pontifical Institute of Mediaeval Studies, 2007.

Louth, Andrew. "The Place of *Theosis* in Orthodox Theology." In Christensen and Wittung, *Partakers of the Divine Nature*, 32–44.

Luther, Martin. *The Freedom of a Christian.* Translated by Mark Tranvik. In *Martin Luther's Basic Theological Writings*, edited by William R. Russell, 403–27. Minneapolis: Fortress, 2012.

Macchia, Frank D. *Jesus the Spirit Baptizer: Christology in Light of Pentecost.* Grand Rapids: Eerdmans, 2018.

Marshall, I. Howard. *Aspects of the Atonement: Cross and Resurrection in the Reconciling of God and Humanity.* London: Paternoster, 2007.

Maximos the Confessor. *On Difficulties in Sacred Scripture: The Responses to Thalassios.* Translated by Maximos Constas. FC. Washington, DC: Catholic University of America Press, 2018.

———. *On Difficulties in the Church Fathers: The* Ambigua. Edited and translated by Nicholas Constas. 2 vols. Dumbarton Oaks Medieval Library. Cambridge, MA: Harvard University Press, 2014.

———. "On the Lord's Prayer." In *The Philokalia*, edited by G. E. H. Palmer, Philip Sherrard, and Kallistos Ware, 2:285–305. London: Faber & Faber, 1981.

McCall, Thomas H. *Forsaken: The Trinity and the Cross, and Why It Matters.* Downers Grove, IL: IVP Academic, 2012.

McClymond, Michael J. *The Devil's Redemption: A New History and Interpretation of Christian Universalism.* 2 vols. Grand Rapids: Baker Academic, 2018.

McCormack, Bruce L. "Participation in God, Yes; Deification, No: Two Modern Protestant Responses to an Ancient Question." In *Orthodox and Modern: Studies in the Theology of Karl Barth*, 235–60. Grand Rapids: Baker Academic, 2008.

———. "'With Loud Cries and Tears': The Humanity of the Son in the Epistle to the Hebrews." In *The Epistle to the Hebrews and Christian Theology*, edited by Richard Bauckham, Daniel R. Driver, Trevor A. Hart, and Nathan MacDonald, 37–68. Grand Rapids: Eerdmans, 2009.

McGrath, Alister E. "The Moral Theory of the Atonement: An Historical and Theological Critique." *Scottish Journal of Theology* 38, no. 2 (1985): 205–20.

McGuckin, J. A. "The Strategic Adaptation of Deification in the Cappadocians." In Christensen and Wittung, *Partakers of the Divine Nature*, 95–114.

McKenny, Gerald. "Freedom, Responsibility, and Moral Agency." In *The Oxford Handbook of Dietrich Bonhoeffer*, edited by Michael Mawson and Philip G. Ziegler, 306–20. Oxford: Oxford University Press, 2019.

McKnight, Scot. "Covenant." In Vanhoozer, *Dictionary for Theological Interpretation of the Bible*, 141–43.

McLay, R. Timothy. *The Use of the Septuagint in New Testament Research*. Grand Rapids: Eerdmans, 2003.

Meconi, David Vincent. *The One Christ: St. Augustine's Theology of Deification*. Washington, DC: Catholic University of America Press, 2018.

Meconi, David, and Carl E. Olson, eds. *Called to Be Children of God: The Catholic Theology of Human Deification*. San Francisco: Ignatius, 2016.

Melanchthon, Philip. *Melanchthon on Christian Doctrine: Loci Communes, 1555*. Edited and translated by Clyde L. Manschreck. Grand Rapids: Baker, 1965.

Menzies, Robert P. *The Development of Early Christian Pneumatology*. London: Sheffield, 1991.

Miley, John. *The Atonement in Christ*. New York: Eaton & Mains, 1907.

Milton, John. *Paradise Lost*. In *John Milton: The Major Works*, edited by Stephen Orgel and Jonathan Goldberg, 355–618. New York: Oxford University Press, 2008.

Moberly, R. W. L. "Exodus, Book of." In Vanhoozer, *Dictionary for Theological Interpretation of the Bible*, 211–16.

———. *Old Testament Theology: Reading the Hebrew Bible as Christian Scripture*. Grand Rapids: Baker Academic, 2013.

Moffitt, David M. *Atonement and the Logic of Resurrection in the Epistle to the Hebrews*. Boston: Brill, 2011.

———. *Rethinking the Atonement: New Perspectives on Jesus's Death, Resurrection, and Ascension*. Grand Rapids: Baker Academic, 2022.

Moltmann, Jürgen. *The Crucified God: The Cross of Christ as the Foundation and Criticism of Christian Theology*. Minneapolis: Fortress, 1993.

Morris, Leon. *The Apostolic Preaching of the Cross*. London: Tyndale, 1955.

———. "Forgiveness." In *Dictionary of Paul and His Letters*, edited by Gerald F. Hawthorne, Ralph P. Martin, and Daniel G. Reid, 311–13. Downers Grove, IL: InterVarsity, 1993.

Murray, Stephen B. *Reclaiming Divine Wrath: A History of a Christian Doctrine and Its Interpretation*. New York: Peter Lang, 2011.

Novotný, Vojtěch. *Cur Homo?* Translated by Pavlína Morgan and Tim Morgan. Prague: Karolinum, 2014.

Oakes, Edward T. "The Internal Logic of Holy Saturday in the Theology of Hans Urs von Balthasar." *International Journal of Systematic Theology* 9, no. 2 (2007): 184–99.

Origen. *Commentary on the Epistle to the Romans*. Translated by Thomas P. Scheck. 2 vols. FC. Washington, DC: Catholic University of America Press, 2001–2.

———. *Homilies on the Psalms*. Translated by Joseph W. Trigg. FC. Washington, DC: Catholic University of America Press, 2020.

———. *On First Principles*. Translated by John Behr. 2 vols. Oxford: Oxford University Press, 2017.

Ortiz, Jared, ed. *Deification in the Latin Patristic Tradition*. Washington, DC: Catholic University of America Press, 2019.

Oxenham, Henry Nutcombe. *The Catholic Doctrine of the Atonement*. London: W. H. Allen, 1881.

Pelikan, Jaroslav. *The Christian Tradition: A History of the Development of Doctrine*. Vol. 3, *The Growth of Medieval Theology (600–1300)*. Chicago: University of Chicago Press, 1978.

Peres, Caio. "Bloodless 'Atonement': An Exegetical, Ritual, and Theological Analysis of Leviticus 5:11–13." *Journal of Hebrew Scriptures* 20 (2021): 1–36.

Petersen, Rodney L. "A Theology of Forgiveness: Terminology, Rhetoric, and the Dialectic of Interfaith Relationships." In Helmick and Petersen, *Forgiveness and Reconciliation*, 3–26.

Peterson, Robert A. *Calvin and the Atonement*. Fearne, Scotland: Christian Focus, 2008.

Peterson, Ryan S. *The Imago Dei as Human Identity: A Theological Interpretation*. Winona Lake, IN: Eisenbrauns, 2016.

Pseudo-Dionysius. *The Complete Works*. Translated by Colm Luibheid. CWS. New York: Paulist Press, 1987.

Pulse, Jeffrey. *Figuring Resurrection: Joseph as a Death and Resurrection Figure in the Old Testament and Second Temple Judaism*. Bellingham, WA: Lexham, 2021.

Purvis, Zachary. *Theology and the University in Nineteenth-Century Germany*. Oxford: Oxford University Press, 2016.

Reichenbach, Bruce R. "Healing View." In *The Nature of the Atonement: Four Views*, edited by James Beilby and Paul R. Eddy, 117–42. Downers Grove, IL: IVP Academic, 2006.

Rigby, Cynthia L. "Forgiveness." In Johnson, *T&T Clark Companion to Atonement*, 493–98.

Rivière, Jean. *The Doctrine of the Atonement: A Historical Essay*. Translated by Luigi Cappadelta. 2 vols. London: Kegan Paul, Trench, Trubner, 1909.

Rosemann, Philipp W. *The Story of a Great Medieval Book: Peter Lombard's Sentences*. North York, Canada: University of Toronto Press, 2007.

Russell, Norman. "A Common Christian Tradition: Deification in the Greek and Latin Fathers." In *Deification in the Latin Patristic Tradition*, edited by Jared Ortiz, 272–94. Washington, DC: Catholic University of America Press, 2019.

———. *The Doctrine of Deification in the Greek Patristic Tradition*. Oxford: Oxford University Press, 2004.

Rutledge, Fleming. *The Crucifixion: Understanding the Death of Jesus Christ*. Grand Rapids: Eerdmans, 2015.

Rutledge, Jonathan C. *Forgiveness and Atonement: Christ's Restorative Sacrifice*. New York: Routledge, 2022.

Sarisky, Darren, ed. *Theologies of Retrieval: An Exploration and Appraisal*. London: T&T Clark, 2017.

Schaff, Philip, ed. *The Creeds of Christendom: With a History and Critical Notes*. Vol. 1, *The History of the Creeds*. Grand Rapids: Baker, 1983.

Schleiermacher, Friedrich. *Brief Outline of Theology as a Field of Study: Revised Translation of the 1811 and 1830 Editions*. Translated by Terrence N. Tice. Louisville: Westminster John Knox, 2011.

———. *Christian Faith: A New Translation and Critical Edition*. Translated by Terrence N. Tice, Catherine L. Kelsey, and Edwina G. Lawler. Louisville: Westminster John Knox, 2016.

Scully, Ellen. *Physicalist Soteriology in Hilary of Poitiers*. Leiden: Brill, 2011.

Shoemaker, David. "The Forgiven." In Warmke, Nelkin, and McKenna, *Forgiveness and Its Moral Dimensions*, 29–56.

Smail, Thomas Allan. *Reflected Glory: The Spirit in Christ and Christians*. London: Hodder & Stoughton, 1975.

Smyth, Geraldine. "Brokenness, Forgiveness, Healing, and Peace in Ireland." In Helmick and Petersen, *Forgiveness and Reconciliation*, 329–60.

Southern, R. W. *Saint Anselm and His Biographer: A Study of Monastic Life and Thought, 1059–c. 1130.* Cambridge: Cambridge University Press, 1963.

Springhart, Heike. "'. . . As We Forgive Those Who Trespass against Us . . .'? Aspects of a Theology of Forgiveness from a Protestant Perspective." In Hahn and Werner, *Mercy and Justice,* 159–72.

Strauss, Mark L. "Jesus and the Spirit in Biblical and Theological Perspective: Messianic Empowering, Saving Wisdom, and the Limits of Biblical Theology." In *The Spirit and Christ in the New Testament and Christian Theology: Essays in Honor of Max Turner,* edited by I. Howard Marshall, Volker Rabens, and Cornelis Bennema, 266–84. Grand Rapids: Eerdmans, 2012.

Stump, Eleonore. *Atonement.* Oxford: Oxford University Press, 2018.

———. "Atonement and Eucharist." In Crisp and Sanders, *Locating Atonement,* 209–25.

Swinburne, Richard. "Forgiving as a Performative Utterance." In Warmke, Nelkin, and McKenna, *Forgiveness and Its Moral Dimensions,* 127–45.

Tan, Carolyn E. L. *The Spirit at the Cross: Exploring a Cruciform Pneumatology; An Investigation into the Holy Spirit's Role at the Cross.* Eugene, OR: Wipf & Stock, 2019.

Tanner, Kathryn. *Christ the Key.* Cambridge: Cambridge University Press, 2010.

Tay, Edwin. "Christ's Priestly Oblation and Intercession: Their Development and Significance in John Owen." In *The Ashgate Research Companion to John Owen's Theology,* edited by Kelly M. Kapic and Mark Jones, 159–70. New York: Routledge, 2012.

Thomas Aquinas. *The Sermon-Conferences of St. Thomas Aquinas on the Apostles' Creed.* Translated by Nicholas Ayo. Notre Dame, IN: University of Notre Dame Press, 1988.

———. *Summa Theologica.* Translated by Fathers of the English Dominican Province. Notre Dame, IN: Christian Classics, 1981.

Torrance, Thomas F. *Atonement: The Person and Work of Christ.* Edited by Robert T. Walker. Downers Grove, IL: InterVarsity, 2009.

———. *The Mediation of Christ.* Colorado Springs: Helmers & Howard, 1992.

———. *Space, Time, and Resurrection.* Grand Rapids: Eerdmans, 1976.

———. *Theology in Reconstruction.* Grand Rapids: Eerdmans, 1966.

———. *The Trinitarian Faith: The Evangelical Theology of the Ancient Catholic Church.* Edinburgh: T&T Clark, 1993.

Traherne, Thomas. *Centuries of Meditations.* Edited by Bertram Dobell. New York: Cosimo Classics, 2007.

Turner, Max. *Power from on High: The Spirit in Israel's Restoration and Witness in Luke-Acts*. London: Sheffield, 1996.

Turretin, Francis. *Institutes of Elenctic Theology*. Vol. 2. Translated by George M. Giger. Edited by James T. Dennison Jr. Phillipsburg: P&R, 1992.

Tutu, Desmond M. Foreword to Helmick and Petersen, *Forgiveness and Reconciliation*, ix–xiv.

van den Brink, Gert. "Hugo Grotius." In Johnson, *T&T Clark Companion to Atonement*, 523–26.

Vanhoozer, Kevin J., ed. *Dictionary for Theological Interpretation of the Bible*. Grand Rapids: Baker Academic, 2005.

———. *The Drama of Doctrine: A Canonical-Linguistic Approach to Christian Theology*. Louisville: Westminster John Knox, 2005.

Venard, Olivier-Thomas. *A Poetic Christ: Thomist Reflections on Scripture, Language and Reality*. Translated by Kenneth Oakes and Francesca Aran Murphy. London: T&T Clark, 2019.

Vermigli, Peter Martyr. *Early Writings: Creed, Scripture, Church*. Translated by Mariano Di Gangi and Joseph C. McLelland. Kirksville, MO: Thomas Jefferson University Press, 1994.

Vidu, Adonis. "Ascension and Pentecost: A View from the Divine Missions." In *Being Saved: Explorations in Human Salvation*, edited by Marc Cortez, Joshua R. Farris, and S. Mark Hamilton, 102–23. London: SCM, 2018.

———. *The Same God Who Works All Things: Inseparable Operations in Trinitarian Theology*. Grand Rapids: Eerdmans, 2021.

Volf, Miroslav. "Divine Violence." *Christian Century*, October 1999. https://www.christiancentury.org/article/2011-07/divine-violence.

———. "Forgiveness, Reconciliation, and Justice: A Christian Contribution to a More Peaceful Social Environment." In Helmick and Petersen, *Forgiveness and Reconciliation*, 27–50.

Warmke, Brandon, Dana Kay Nelkin, and Michael McKenna, eds. *Forgiveness and Its Moral Dimensions*. Oxford: Oxford University Press, 2021.

———. "Forgiveness: An Introduction." In Warmke, Nelkin, and McKenna, *Forgiveness and Its Moral Dimensions*, 1–28.

Watson, Francis. "Paul and Scripture." In *The Oxford Handbook of Pauline Studies*, edited by Matthew V. Novenson and R. Barry Matlock, 357–70. Oxford: Oxford University Press, 2022.

Webster, John. *Confessing God: Essays in Christian Dogmatics II*. London: T&T Clark, 2005.

———. *The Culture of Theology*. Edited by Ivor J. Davidson and Alden C. McCray. Grand Rapids: Baker Academic, 2019.

———. *God without Measure: Working Papers in Christian Theology*. 2 vols. New York: T&T Clark, 2016.

———. *Holiness*. London: SCM, 2003.

———. *Holy Scripture: A Dogmatic Sketch*. New York: Cambridge University Press, 2003.

———. "The Identity of the Holy Spirit: A Problem in Trinitarian Theology." *Themelios* 9, no. 1 (1983): 4–7.

———. "Intellectual Patience." In *God without Measure*, 2:173–88.

———. "'It Was the Will of the Lord to Bruise Him': Soteriology and the Doctrine of God." In *God of Salvation: Soteriology in Theological Perspective*, edited by Ivor J. Davidson and Murray A. Rae, 15–34. Burlington, VT: Ashgate, 2011.

———. "*Non ex aequo*: God's Relation to Creatures." In *God without Measure*, 1:115–26.

———. "Theologies of Retrieval." In *The Oxford Handbook of Systematic Theology*, edited by John Webster, Kathryn Tanner, and Iain Torrance, 583–99. New York: Oxford University Press, 2007.

———. *Word and Church: Essays in Christian Dogmatics*. New York: T&T Clark, 2001.

Wendte, Martin. "Ferdinand Christian Baur: A Historically Informed Idealist of a Distinctive Kind." In Bauspiess, Landmesser, and Lincicum, *Ferdinand Christian Baur and the History of Early Christianity*, 67–80.

William of Auvergne. *The Treatise on the Reasons Why God Became Man*. In *Selected Spiritual Writings*, translated by Roland J. Teske, 19–62. Toronto: Pontifical Institute of Mediaeval Studies, 2011.

Wright, Christopher J. H. "Atonement in the Old Testament." In *The Atonement Debate: Papers from the London Symposium on the Theology of Atonement*, edited by Derek Tidball, David Hilborn, and Justin Thacker, 69–82. Grand Rapids: Zondervan, 2008.

———. *Knowing the Holy Spirit through the Old Testament*. Downers Grove, IL: IVP Academic, 2006.

Wright, N. T. *The Climax of the Covenant: Christ and the Law in Pauline Theology*. Minneapolis: Fortress, 1992.

———. *The Day the Revolution Began: Reconsidering the Meaning of Jesus's Crucifixion*. New York: HarperCollins, 2016.

———. *Jesus and the Victory of God*. Minneapolis: Fortress, 1996.

———. *The New Testament and the People of God*. Minneapolis: Fortress, 1992.

———. *Paul and the Faithfulness of God*. 2 vols. Minneapolis: Fortress, 2013.

Wynne, Jeremy J. *Wrath among the Perfections of God's Life*. New York: T&T Clark, 2010.

Yang, Eric T., and Stephen T. Davis. "Atonement and the Wrath of God." In Crisp and Sanders, *Locating Atonement*, 154–67.

Young, Frances M. *Construing the Cross: Type, Sign, Symbol, Word, Action*. Eugene, OR: Cascade Books, 2015.

———. "The 'Mind' of Scripture: Theological Readings of the Bible in the Fathers." *International Journal of Systematic Theology* 7, no. 2 (2005): 126–41.

Zachhuber, Johannes. "The Absoluteness of Christianity and the Relativity of All History: Two Strands in Ferdinand Christian Baur's Thought." In Bauspiess, Landmesser, and Lincicum, *Ferdinand Christian Baur and the History of Early Christianity*, 287–304.

———. "The Historical Turn." In *The Oxford Handbook of Nineteenth-Century Christian Thought*, edited by Joel D. S. Rasmussen, Judith Wolfe, and Johannes Zachhuber, 53–71. Oxford: Oxford University Press, 2017.

Zwingli, Ulrich. *On Providence and Other Essays*. Edited by William John Hinke. Durham, NC: Labyrinth, 1983.

Author Index

Scripture Index

Subject Index